THE BALL & CHAIN

a guide to hammer throwing

THE BALL & CHAIN

a guide to hammer throwing

G. MARTIN BINGISSER

Published by HMMR Media LLC
HMMR Media LLC
4230 137th Avenue NE
Bellevue, WA 98005
www.hmmrmedia.com

Copyright © 2015 by Glen Martin Bingisser

All rights reserved. This book or any portion thereof may not be reproduced or used in any form without prior written consent from the publisher.

First published, 2015
ISBN: 978-0-9915361-0-8

Printed in the United States of America
10 9 8 7 6 5 4 3 2 1

Set in Minion Pro

*for my parents, who have wholeheartedly
supported my devotion to this sport*

CONTENTS

Introduction — ix

PART I // STARTING TO THROW — 1
   1 // The Philosophy of Hammer Throwing — 3
   2 // Talent Identification — 7
   3 // Learning to Throw — 15

PART II // HAMMER THROW TECHNIQUE — 23
   4 // Three Levels of Technique — 25
   5 // The Basic Science of Hammer Throwing — 29
   6 // The Positions — 35
   7 // The Movements — 45
   8 // Coaching — 51

PART III // ADVANCED TECHNIQUE — 59
   9 // Common Problems and Solutions — 61
   10 // Biomechanics — 69

PART IV // TRAINING — 75
   11 // Exercise Selection — 77
   12 // Specific Developmental Exercises — 83

13 // Throwing as Training	91
14 // Advanced Training Concepts	97

EPILOGUE   **107**

References and Credits   111

Acknowledgements   115

About the Author   117

INTRODUCTION

There is no doubt that the hammer throw is one of the most addicting events in track and field. The feeling you get when throwing is ineffable, but its effect isn't. After just one attempt, athletes are sucked into the sport.

If you are a hammer thrower reading this book, there is a high likelihood you already suffer from this addiction. There are simply few other reasons you would choose to compete in the most obscure track and field event and then dedicate your free time to reading about it. And if you are new to the event, consider yourself warned.

I've had a few teammates that continued to jump, sprint, or run well after they had lost their love for the event. They only continued because they were good, could make a few bucks, and had reached a certain level of recognition. These people don't exist in the hammer throw. There is little money or recognition. Hammer throwers compete for love and are driven by this addiction.

An addiction is simply a compulsion to do something, in spite of potentially negative consequences. In my experience, there are both good addictions and bad addictions. The only difference is that with good ones, there are more positive than negative consequences. Identifying where hammer throwing falls in this spectrum is not always an easy task. On the one hand,

THE BALL & CHAIN

it will take your money; it will take your time; and it can make even the most obscure muscles in your body ache for weeks on end. But it keeps you fit; it gives you a challenge; and, most importantly, it brings you into a community. For me, the net balance is positive.

I am not the world's greatest coach. It is a stretch to even call myself an expert. What I am is an addict. This has led me around the world for the past decade to learn from the most successful coaches and athletes that have ever touched a hammer. This book is a collection of what I have learned, both technical and philosophical.

Each part of this book tackles an important topic in hammer throwing, from beginning to throw to understanding hammer throw technique, refining that technique, and then assembling a holistic training plan. But before we start discussing the details of hammer throwing, it is helpful to talk about what it takes to be a hammer thrower and my first experience with the event. Only special athletes fit into the mold of a hammer thrower and without a good fit, the rest of the book may be useless.

• • •

As with most throwers, I can vividly recall my first introduction to the hammer. I was a budding young 15-year-old shot putter when I went to watch a collegiate track meet at the University of Washington. The star attraction of the meet was All-American shot put and discus thrower Ben Lindsey. As I walked towards the shot put ring, I was stopped in my tracks by a loud clang that left my ears ringing. It was as if Thor himself used all his force to ring a gigantic gong with his hammer. My neck whipped around to identify the source and saw that someone had thrown a hammer into the metal cage supports. I went in for a closer look.

I had no idea this was a bad throw. Like many people, I am surprised by sudden loud noises. But it didn't matter to me. After the bang I stayed to watch the throws that actually made it out of the cage. This impressed me even more. I never did end up making it over to see Lindsey throw that day.

Introduction

• • •

One thing that impressed me was that the athletes in the hammer throw competition came in all shapes and sizes. Some were tall; others were not. Some looked like bodybuilders and others looked like plumbers or even distance runners. I could see that it was a democratic event, open to anyone. I didn't know exactly what it required, but I was instantly confident that I could be good at it.

In the nearly 15 years since then, I have learned first-hand the traits that the hammer throw requires. Athletic talent is helpful, but it comes in many varieties. What hammer throwers all have in common are talents that aren't just found in muscles. Specifically, these traits are patience, passion, and perseverance.

Patience. Back in 2006, 21-year-old Donald Thomas accepted a friend's dare to clear six-and-a-half feet in the high jump. The challenge may not seem like much for an elite athlete, but Thomas was not a high jumper. He was a point guard for the small Lindenwood University Lions in St. Charles, Missouri. Both men went to the gym where Thomas not only cleared the height, but raised the bar and then easily jumped over seven feet. Two days later he competed in his first track meet and cleared 2.22 meters (7 feet 3.25 inches) in tennis shoes.

A little more than a year later Thomas improved to 2.35 meters (7 feet 8.5 inches), was crowned the world champion, and became a favorite to win the event at the following year's Olympics in Beijing. Clearly Thomas had a natural jumping ability. Nothing else could explain how he was able to progress from a beginner to a world-class jumper in just two days. This is a story that you hear again and again from many different sports. However, you will never hear of it happening in the hammer throw.

The youngest world champion in the hammer throw was Sergey Litvinov, who won his first title at age 25 after more than a decade of focused hammer throw training. Koji Murofushi, at nearly 37-years-old and three decades after he first picked up a hammer, finally won his first world title in 2011. World record holder Yuriy Sedykh also had to wait until age 36 for his first world championship.

My point is that the Donald Thomas story just doesn't happen in the hammer throw. The hammer throw is not a natural movement; no one can just pick one up for the first time and throw 80 meters. It takes years or even decades to build the technique and strength needed to throw that far. In other words, it takes patience.

A lack of patience normally stops potential hammer throwers before they even start the event. Several years ago I had the chance to observe a top high school shot putter try the hammer for the first time. While he routinely beat throwers by three meters (10 feet) in high school shot put competitions, his coach thought that the hammer might be a better long-term fit for his slender build. He only lasted two sessions before giving up because he didn't like the fact that he could not yet complete a full throw. It also didn't help that less talented athletes were kicking his ass. The hammer throw requires the patience to sacrifice both time and humility in the short term in return for results in the long term. Not everyone can endure years of hard work, waiting for a reward that lies on the distant horizon. This is why the best hammer throwers have patience.

Passion. Star basketball and football players usually make millions of dollars. After his world record, Usain Bolt was on front pages around the world. Even the occasional shot putter can make it on *The Tonight Show*. Hammer throwers likely will never attain such fame or fortune.

I've had former teammates that continue to run and jump after college not because they have a passion to succeed, but because they were good and could make a living in the sport. You won't find these people in the hammer throw precisely because the event will not bring fame or fortune. Those types of athletes simply leave the sport; only those who are passionate continue.

An athlete cannot have too much passion and, as a coach, I always find it preferable to have an athlete that you need to hold back rather than motivate. These are the athletes who want to train through a broken bone, rather than the athlete that asks for a week off to recover from a stuffy nose. Passion can make an athlete do stupid things sometimes, but a coach can always tell an athlete to stop before the passion makes things worse. It is simply important that they have passion since motivating an apathetic athlete is nearly impossible.

Perseverance. The best coaches and throwers I've met find a way to make things work, no matter the situation. I always joke that one of the best traits a hammer thrower can have is the ability to jump over fences. With limited places to train, every hammer thrower eventually has to do this in his or her career to get some training done. I've often thrown in the pitch black dead of night just to find a time and place to train. One time I even attached glow sticks to my hammer in order to help find where it landed in the field. (This experiment failed once the glow sticks exploded, giving the grass a fluorescent glow.) My coach, Anatoliy Bondarchuk, will have people throw hunks of metal with a wire attached if no hammer is to be found. The best throwers do not complain; they just persevere and make the most of the situation.

Also, hammer throwers can't just sit around and wait for someone to come and help them out, since that person will likely never arrive. They often have to work full time jobs, pay for their own training and travel expenses, and struggle to find the support they need to succeed. They have to rely on their perseverance to carry them.

Patience, passion, and perseverance are all related. They are all manifestations of this addiction. Patience comes from knowing something is so good that it is worth the wait. Passion is the internal desire that fuels you to chase it. Perseverance pushes you to act upon the desire and knock down anything in your way to chase it.

. . .

While watching that first hammer competition got me interested in the event, I actually didn't become addicted until later. When I got home that day I starting looking for meets that might offer the hammer throw. Eventually, I found one and registered for it. The next step was to practice. I assembled my own version of a hammer using a shot put and a canvas bag with handles. With an online video of Yuriy Sedykh's world record as my guide, I proceeded to try a few throws before the bag broke. After that I just waited for the competition, where I would be able to get my hands on a real hammer for the first time.

Two months later, my family and I made the 300-mile drive east to an isolated field in rural Cheney, Washington, for my first meet. I lied about my experience to get into the meet. One of the fathers took me aside and showed me enough so that I wouldn't hurt myself or anyone else. I threw around 30 meters that day from a standing position with just a few winds. I might have won a medal against the small field. This is when my addiction began.

PART I //

STARTING TO THROW

1 // THE PHILOSOPHY OF HAMMER THROWING

In the lead up to the 2011 US Track and Field Championships, *New York Times* reporter Isolde Raftery published a feature article on the hammer throw. As Raftery accurately describes it, most fans must leave the stadium and get out a map to find the hammer competition. As hard as it is for fans to find the event, it is even more difficult for athletes to make a living with it. Yet all is not lost:

> Rather than being bitter, American hammer throwers seem introspective. They wax poetic about physics, rhythm and kamiwaza—the Japanese word for divine work or superhuman feat.[1]

It's a good observation. Analytic and philosophical types are overrepresented in the hammer throw. There are, of course, throwers of all backgrounds, but the nature of the event attracts the inquisitive. We hammer throwers are constantly searching for the key to unlocking a better throw. All throwers need a philosophy. A philosophy is a big concept. Rather than just being a normal idea or opinion, a philosophy can be a guiding life principle. It can lead you to the right answer or the wrong answer, the good action or the bad one.

THE BALL & CHAIN

The hammer throw itself is hardly a life philosophy. While the event has many redeeming values—after all it helped turn me from a fat, failing, high school student into a successful international athlete and attorney—these are just by-products. People don't pick up a hammer to change their life; they pick it up for fun or for the challenge. When it comes down to it, we are just hurling a hunk of metal into a field and that is hard to defend as a life philosophy.

While the hammer throw is not a philosophy, the way you approach it does have its own philosophy. Thus, I want to explain the philosophy of hammer throwing. This is the meaning of the event instead of the meaning of life; a guide to your training instead of a guide to your moral decisions. The philosophy of hammer throwing is the underlying principle to which the event always returns.

• • •

Sometimes near the end of a coaching session, when everything I have tried has failed to help my athlete, I will pull him or her aside, look straight into his or her eyes and say, "On this last throw you just need to maximize the distance between you and where the ball lands." After a second or two of confusion, the athlete realizes I just told them to throw farther.

I normally use this as a joke since I can't think of anything that is actually helpful and if nothing else a small laugh may help the athlete relax. But in the end, what I'm saying is true; after all that's the goal of hammer throwing, isn't it? We don't aim to throw beautifully; we aim to throw far.

Having a goal like this is part of a philosophy, but not all of it. Guiding a life to do "good" means nothing unless you know what good is. The same goes with hammer throwing. You may want to throw far, but that is useless unless you know how to do it.

In the *New York Times* article, 1996 Olympic silver medalist Lance Deal told Raftery, "The secret of the hammer is the pendulum." Another person identified the abstract concept of "the system." I've met many coaches who say strength is the key to long throws. Others simply credit genetics and natural talent.

My philosophy of hammer throwing is speed. As I'll explain in Chapter 5, the distance of a throw is largely determined by the speed the hammer is traveling when it is released. Speed is responsible for every good throw; without it the hammer will not fly far. Adopting this philosophy will assist you in finding where speed comes from and then focus on it throughout training. Getting stronger, improving technique, and improving rhythm all help the hammer go faster, and thus farther.

Once you adopt this philosophy, it affects your whole outlook on training. Rather than asking what exercises will make you stronger, you really have to look at what type of strength will make the ball go faster and how technique, rhythm, and other concepts can help accelerate the hammer. You have to question everything and see how it comes back to speed.

These questions may seem obvious, but I cannot tell you how often they are overlooked by even the best coaches and athletes.

Speed is the underlying theme of this book, but it is not the only approach to the hammer throw that works. Whatever your philosophy is, keep it in mind throughout each chapter.

2 // TALENT IDENTIFICATION

While every hammer thrower needs to get the hammer moving fast, there are many ways to do it and many body types that can be successful at it. The hammer throw is perhaps the most egalitarian event in track and field even though it doesn't appear so on the surface.

It is true that the top hammer throwers tend to have similar characteristics in size and strength. For example, at the London Olympics nearly all of the finalists in the men's hammer throw were very close to 1.88 meters tall (6 feet 2 inches). But unlike in other events, exceptions to the prototypical hammer thrower are common.

Athens Olympic champion Koji Murofushi first threw 80 meters when he weighed less than 90 kilograms (200 pounds), and other Olympians have topped the scales at over 150 kilograms (330 pounds). Pavel Ryepin of the Soviet Union also threw over 77 meters at just 1.70 meters tall (5 feet 7 inches), while still others have surpassed that distance at a height of over 2.05 meters (6 feet 9 inches). I do not think another event has seen such a range in athletes attaining such a high level of success.

The determining factor is that all of these athletes were willing to put in the necessary effort to reach a world-class level. Unlike some events, the hammer throw will reward you for effort as much as talent. Not everyone may be capable of winning a medal, but they can reach a high level if they commit wholeheartedly. Since the average hammer thrower at the London Olympics was over 30-years-old, there is plenty of time for the hard work to pay dividends.

Despite these differences, physical talent still exists in the hammer throw. Whether you like it or not, some athletes are genetically predisposed to being good hammer throwers, and every coach I know is looking for ways to identify these athletes. There are several methods coaches can use to look for talent.

• • •

Explosiveness. Several tests exist to look at the explosiveness of an athlete. The hammer throw is about speed, and to get that speed an athlete obviously needs to be able to generate great amounts of power. Exercises like the overhead shot put or a 30-meter sprint can help measure this. For this reason, many coaches I know use a form of the Max Jones Quad Test to measure explosiveness.[2] In essence, this is a test of power where points are added up in four events: a 30-meter sprint, the overhead shot put throw, standing long jump, and standing triple jump.

However, the test is not perfect. I was first introduced to this test during my freshman year of college by coach Glenn McAtee, and even he recognizes its shortcomings. As he told me recently, "[The test] is not very hammer specific or even throws specific. Rarely are your best throwers also your best quadrathletes." While a good score may be indicative of general athletic talent, the top score does not mean that the athlete has the most hammer throw talent.

Coordination. Another way to go about identifying talent is to look at coordination, a key element in the hammer throw. McAtee suggested having athletes close their eyes and turn around 10 times before opening their eyes and walking forward to a point 10 meters away. Deviations of less than 10 degrees are acceptable.

Several years ago at a conference, former Olympic champion and Soviet national coach Anatoliy Bondarchuk mentioned a similar approach. In response to a question about Soviet talent identification methods, he responded along the lines of, "[I]t was simple: if you could run fast we made you a sprinter, if you could jump high we made you a jumper, and if you could throw far we made you a thrower." Have an athlete throw a hammer, and see how natural they look in their first attempts.

Personally, I have someone just pick up and throw a hammer or walk around in circles with the hammer. I've found that those who have a natural instinct to relax and push the hammer, not surprisingly, turn out to be better hammer throwers no matter how far they throw on the first day. They have an intuitive sense of how to add speed to the hammer. Kids who force the throws may throw farther at first, but it can be difficult to teach them to truly relax and work with the hammer, a skill needed to reach an elite level.

Holistic Approach. Another group of coaches take a more holistic approach by looking at a variety of factors including explosiveness, coordination, and non-physical attributes. A new talent identification system used by the Swiss Olympic Association gives young athletes points based on competition results and both sport-specific and general motor tests. In addition, points are given based on interviews with the athlete to assess motivation, family situation, and stage of physical development. These last factors should not be underestimated since they consider not just the athlete's current results but their potential for growth, which is the ultimate goal.

Many factors can be measured to identify talent, and all of them provide valuable information to the coach. When in doubt, more data and more input can be more helpful. Due to the complexity of the hammer throw, there is no one measure that can quickly pinpoint an athlete's potential.

THE BALL & CHAIN

• • •

While most standard talent identification tests are no doubt helpful, their shortcoming is that they only provide a single snapshot of the situation. Talent, however, is multi-dimensional. It is not just where the athlete is currently, but how easily he will get to where he needs to be. This latter part is more difficult to measure in a test.

The best definition of talent was given to me by Anatoliy Bondarchuk:

> Talent of athletes is determined by . . . the number of periods of development of sports form over which his increases can be observed. In champions, it is significantly greater than in athletes in which an increase in sports achievements stopped at the level of his first sports classification.[3]

His athlete, and two-time Olympic hammer throw medallist Jüri Tamm, spelled it out at a more practical level. As he defined it:

> Talent is the person that can develop longer than others. It is not the person who after two months can throw 60 meters. Adaptation is the biggest problem in our world. The body always wants to stay where it is at, since that is more comfortable. The person that can keep developing is more talented.[4]

Coaches tend to think that the athlete who throws well quickly will be the best in the end. This assumption ignores the role of talent in athlete development. Athlete development depends as much on talent as it does on coaching, support, and other factors. If you give two athletes the same athlete program, it will likely work better or continue working longer for one of the athletes. This athlete, who might not have been the best at the start, has more talent in the sense that they can more easily be trained to a higher level. Amplify these results over a decade of training, and suddenly this athlete is beating the other athlete by a large margin. This type of talent plays a huge role, but is hard to measure at the start of an athlete's career since it involves seeing how the athlete reacts over time.

The assumption that athletes who throw farther more quickly will be the best is also simply incorrect. Over the last few decades, history confirms that only a few of the best youth throwers turned into the best elite throwers. In early 2012, I compiled an analysis of the results from all the World Junior and World Youth Championships from 1998 to 2006. These athletes were the best young throwers at their time and had reached the prime of their careers. If the best young athletes turn into the best elite athletes, then the youth and junior champions would also be among the world's best when they reached their prime. But after analyzing how their careers progressed, both youth and junior success had a very poor correlation to adult success.

The results showed that only 29 percent of the men that made the World Junior final continued on to even compete at the World Championships in the future. A typical year was 2002, where only two of 12 male finalists from 2002 World Junior Championships ever went on to qualify for a World Championship or Olympic team.

The women's results were slightly better, likely due to the fact that junior women and elite women both throw the 4-kilogram hammer (i.e., men could be hampered by the change in weight). At the youth level for both men and women, the numbers were nearly 50 percent (50%) lower by every measurement, meaning there was even less connection between youth and adult success.

When the standard of success is raised, the numbers were even lower: only seven percent (7%) of those World Junior finalists ever went on to make an Olympic Final. It was even more rare for a youth or junior finalist to go on and win a World Championship or Olympic medal. In fact, Dylan Armstrong's shot put silver medal at the 2011 World Championship meant that male world junior hammer throw finalists (Armstrong placed second in the hammer at the 2000 World Juniors) have won the same number of World Championship medals in the shot put as the hammer throw. Again, the women have been much more successful in this area, but most of the medals were before 2004 when the event was relatively new and there were not as many older athletes to compete against.

My favorite example is that of Primož Kozmus of Slovenia. As a junior in 1998, he failed to break 70 meters with the 6-kilogram hammer, but he had the other factors needed to succeed and ended up becoming an Olympic and World champion 10 years later against a strong field. Among his competition in 2008 was Olli-Pekka Karjalainen of Finland, the World Junior champion from 1998, who had already broken 78 meters with the heavier 7.26-kilogram hammer as a junior. At the Beijing Olympics, he threw no further. Who would have predicted that Kozmus would be the better thrower ten years later? But that's the point. Predicting who will be the best in the world in a decade is a hard thing to do, no matter what the test.

Why is this the case? Maybe these athletes lacked the talent for development discussed above and were not physically able to continue to develop into better throwers. Maybe the lack of early success led their competitors to train harder and surpass them. Maybe they just burned out. Perhaps they had bad luck with injuries, not enough support to develop their talent further, or other external factors impacting their progress. The only thing we know is that predicting success is not that simple because tests and indicators often look at a static point in time rather than the potential for future development.

• • •

Using Bondarchuk's definition, the only way to truly identify talent is to give everyone a chance. Then, wait and see who continues to develop. Tests cannot hurt, but I see their role primarily in the area of dividing limited funding and resources among groups. As coaches, we should be active recruiters to get anyone we can involved in our sport. I have never turned away a thrower and doubt I ever will, as long as they work hard and do not disrupt my training group. Recruit as many throwers as possible and see who has the desire and ability to keep improving. This is the only way to make sure that the truly talented athletes are not overlooked.

3 // LEARNING TO THROW

Looking back, I actually learned to throw the hammer twice, and the first time I was unsuccessful. As mentioned in the Introduction, I taught myself to throw the hammer at age 15 by playing around with it after shot put training was finished. Even after three years of training a few times a month, I was still using just one or two turns in competitions and had no concept of what the event was about. I definitely was hooked, but I had no idea how to throw yet.

When I was 18, I met former Olympic champion Harold Connolly and promptly began learning all over again under his guidance. This time I had a plan. For weeks on end I did drill after drill, but did not take one throw. Even after I began throwing again, drills took up a significant part of my training for the next four years. Connolly's theory was to perfect the basics of technique before ever entering the ring. He had molded his ideas based on his 50 years in the sport and had just finished a guidebook for beginners that laid out the plan in detail. I was one of his guinea pigs.

Through Connolly's method I developed great footwork, but in hindsight that isn't where my focus should have been. My technical problems, to this day, relate to my rhythm and how to properly accelerate the hammer.

THE BALL & CHAIN

Drills can't replicate the true rhythm of a throw. Doing dozens of turns in a row might lead to good footwork, but the forces the athlete most confront and the rhythm will never match those of a normal throw. Throwing should have also been my focus in the beginning.

My current approach to coaching new throwers was strongly influenced by my current coach and another former Olympic champion, Bondarchuk. He focuses on getting a thrower to complete a full throw as quickly as possible, and then works on slowly refining their technique. This way, the beginner can immediately feel the forces of a real throw and learn how to control them.

• • •

There is a constant debate over which of these methods is the best method for teaching the hammer. One critic of the "throw first" method told me that it is not possible to learn to throw without first learning the pieces of the throw. No one has been able to more coherently state my response to this opinion than my friend, Pacific Lutheran University coach Dan Haakenson. As Haakenson told me:

> I would venture to say exactly the opposite. Only after someone has begun to understand what a good throw feels like can they grasp the concept of the importance of winding and footwork.

In my opinion, there are advantages and disadvantages to starting with drills and starting with throws. Learning the throw in pieces can destroy the concept of unity in the throw, where all the pieces have to work together. But learning to throw first can lead to inappropriately pulling the hammer if the athlete's instincts are not controlled. What is important is that the athlete learns under the watchful eye of a knowledgeable coach so that he or she does not learn bad habits that can take a career to fix. I have often trained alone in my career and that, rather than the method I used to learn the hammer, caused more of my technical problems.

Starting to Throw

I prefer teaching the "throw first" method not as much for pedagogical reasons, but because it is also more fun for athletes. Convincing a young athlete to try an event for weeks without actually throwing is a bit unrealistic. No one would ever expect a new baseball player to endure training for weeks before getting the chance to hit their first pitch. Even if you can maintain their attention for that long, the process makes it harder for them to fall in love with the event. The faster you get them to throw, the faster they'll become hooked.

This chapter outlines the "throw first" method. After giving a brief overview of the equipment needed to throw and the most important rules, I will outline how to teach the hammer throw in three simple steps.

• • •

First things first, you need some equipment and facilities before you even begin to throw:

A ring and cage. Just as basketball uses a court, the hammer throw has a ring and cage. This is where the work takes place. The hammer is thrown from a ring 2.135 meters (7 feet) in diameter. This is slightly smaller than a discus ring, but for training purposes a discus ring will work just fine. The ring is then surrounded by a cage made of netting. In order to contain longer and more powerful throws, a hammer cage is typically larger than a discus cage, but for training purposes, a discus cage should also be sufficient to protect you and other spectators from potentially errant throws. However, a taller cage with movable doors may be required for competitions.

A field. The ring and cage is only half of the playing field. The hammer also needs a place to land, and finding one can be difficult since the hammer causes divots and can make enemies out of groundskeepers. Thankfully beginning throwers will not be throwing far enough to do much damage and can throw into almost any field with a discus cage. As throwers advance, it will be important to find a facility that allows the hammer throw. Repeated use can make some fields unusable for other sports, so a dedicated throwing field is preferable to multi-purpose fields. In competitions, a 34.92-degree sector must also be marked on the field.

A hammer. This is what you throw and, despite the jokes you will hear throughout your throwing career, it bears little resemblance to a carpenter's hammer. The hammer itself is made up of three parts: a metal ball, a steel wire, and a handle. While the standard hammer weights are 7.26 kilograms (16 pounds) for men and 4 kilograms (8.8 pounds) for women, both younger and older athletes compete with lighter implements. There are also detailed regulations regarding the handle and wire. A complete list of the appropriate weight and specifications for each age group can be found in Table 1. Hammers can be ordered from all track and field suppliers or found through a quick internet search.

If possible, it is best to learn with a lighter than competition weight hammer since it is easier to relax and there is less tendency to force the implement. Shorter hammers are also easier to learn with since they let the athlete feel the implement better and negate the fear of hitting the ground with the hammer.

A glove. A glove is not necessary for beginners, but throwers will quickly want one as they become more advanced and the force of the throw pulls more on their hands. Hammer throw gloves are available for purchase from track and field suppliers, but a leather gardening glove will also work just fine for beginners. In competition, throwers must use a glove which exposes the fingertips. The hammer glove is worn on the left hand for right-handed throwers.

A pair of shoes. Like a glove, hammer throwing shoes are not necessary for beginners. Shoes with a flat rubber sole, minimal heel, and limited grip can work as a good substitute. However, hammer or discus throwing shoes are helpful in executing the footwork, especially as a thrower reaches an intermediate level.

Starting to Throw

TABLE 1: HAMMER SPECIFICATIONS			
Implement Weight (kg)	Age Groups	Maximum Length (mm)	Minimum Ball Diameter (mm)
2	≥ 75 and older Women	1195	76
3	< 18 Girls; 50-74 Women; ≥ 80 Men	1195	85
4	18-50 Women, 70-79 Men	1195	95
5	< 18 Boys, 60-69 Men	1200	100
5.45	US/Canada High School Boys	1200	100
6	< 20 Boys, 50-59 Men	1215	105
7.26	20-49 Men	1215	110

• • •

As with any sport, the hammer throw also has rules and it is helpful to have a brief overview of the rules before stepping into the ring.[5]

A thrower may enter the ring from any direction, but they must stay within the ring during the throw for it to be considered a valid throw. After releasing the throw and letting it land in the sector, they must also exit from the back half. If the hammer happens to break during a throw, the athlete can be awarded a replacement throw. The implement is also not limited to staying in the circle the same way the athlete is. The thrower, for example, can also start their attempt with the hammer on the ground outside the circle. And while the athlete must stay in the circle, the hammer is allowed to hit the ground during the throw without making the attempt invalid.

• • •

Step 1: Pick up the hammer. A right-handed thrower should pick up the hammer with his/her left hand, gripping it between the first and second joint of the fingers. The right hand should be placed on top of (i.e., around) the left hand with the thumbs pointing up.

THE BALL & CHAIN

• • •

Step 2: Wind and release the hammer. The hammer throw can be hard for beginners to learn when coaches overcomplicate it. When a coach keeps it simple, learning to throw will not only be more fun for the athlete, but also easier for the coach.

To wind the hammer, the athlete should face away from the landing area and swing the hammer around the head counter clockwise. The coach should remind the athlete to keep the arms and upper body relaxed, and bend the arms while the hammer goes behind the head, but always keep them straight and long while in front of the body. Have the athlete take two winds and then release the hammer over their shoulder into the field behind him. When releasing, make sure the feet stay on the ground while the athlete simply lets go of the hammer at the appropriate time.

An athlete should take multiple throws like this while the coach begins to tinker with the technique on each attempt. The first concept an athlete should learn is when to "push" or "accelerate" the hammer. During each wind, the athlete should add a little speed to the hammer by actively accelerating the hammer from the end of the second wind until the hammer is directly in front of the athlete. Once the hammer is directly in front of the athlete, it is too late to accelerate. The athlete should also make sure the hammer stays in front of the body and the athlete is not leading and dragging the hammer throughout the throw. Doing this also requires the shoulders to turn back with the hammer in each wind.

The other elements of the throw (e.g., proper orbit, balance, etc.) will begin to fall into place with lots of repetitions; the coach should not address these elements at this time since it can overwhelm the athlete.

• • •

Step 3: Wind, turn, and release. Soon the athlete will become very comfortable with winding and releasing. The coach must determine when the athlete is ready to move on to the next step. For some athletes, this takes less than one practice session, but for others, it can be multiple sessions. Before the athlete begins to turn, he or she should take a few more winds and releases while flexing the ankle to bring the toes closer to the shin (i.e. dorsiflexion) prior to the release. The athlete should begin to turn on the left heel, as the hammer comes around in front of him. However, despite this difference, the athlete will release the hammer without executing a turn. Still, the simple act of dorsiflexing the foot will get him or her used to transferring his or her weight to the heel, which is the first step of a complete turn.

When an athlete begins to try a real turn, the coach should focus on the athlete's upper body. Focusing on footwork can easily confuse most beginners and promote poor technique. Have the athlete perform normal winds, with a focus on accelerating the hammer at the proper times. On the second wind, the athlete will accelerate the hammer around to the left and let the hammer turn the athlete. If the athlete has flexed the foot properly, he/she will turn around with the hammer beginning on the heel of the left foot.

Athletes must then pick up the right foot after a quarter turn. Midway through the turn, the athlete simply puts the right foot down to complete the turn. These points will come almost naturally if the athlete focuses more on accelerating the hammer and allowing the hammer to turn the body rather than the body turning the hammer. The body will then find these positions on its own.

The athlete's first throw should be with just one turn so that he/she can become comfortable with the feeling of the hammer while turning and transitioning from turning to releasing. After the thrower becomes comfortable with one turn, he/she should progress to three turns. Most elite throwers use three or four turns, so reaching this stage quickly will help one's development. As progress is made, the coach should continue to tinker with technique and work on identifying and correcting any errors.

THE BALL & CHAIN

· · ·

It may not be this simple in practice, but teaching the hammer can definitely be easier than many people make it out to be. Despite being a complex event, a simple approach is what is needed to start athletes on the path to success.

PART II //

HAMMER THROW TECHNIQUE

4 // THREE LEVELS OF TECHNIQUE

One of the easiest things to do as a coach is to identify technical flaws. Doing so is important, but it requires little experience, interpersonal skills, or analysis. But finding the problem is not the same as fixing it. Coaching is a much more holistic endeavor, and identifying technical problems is just the beginning of a three-level process for improving technique that applies not only to the hammer throw, but to all technical events and sports.

The first level is the easiest: analyzing positions. After that comes analyzing the movements that connect the positions. And finally, a coach has to figure out a way to get an athlete to achieve both the desired positions and movements. While there is some overlap of these levels, they are mostly distinct, requiring a separate approach and thought process. The only thing each step has in common is that they all require the coach to understand the basics elements of hammer throwing.

・・・

The Positions. While there is not a one-size-fits-all, perfect technique in the hammer throw, there are certain things that all top throwers have in common and that all throwers should strive to achieve. Throwers come in different shapes and sizes. They have different strengths and weaknesses.

THE BALL & CHAIN

They have to counter and work with different forces. This will give each thrower distinctive characteristics in their style. However, there will still be more in common than is different. For example, in the hammer throw the arms should be straight, body weight should be balanced, and so on.

This level can be completed through a frame-by-frame video analysis of the positions reached during each part of the throw. Looking at each frame quickly lets you know whether the athlete is generally doing things correctly. And once you know the individual style your athlete is aiming for, you can also bring this into the position analysis.

• • •

The Movements. What takes technique to the next level is what you do with those positions. It is generally accepted that a long double support phase, i.e., the period of time during the throw with both feet on the ground, is a sign of good technique. Now let's say an athlete starts double support early. That's a good start, but it won't convert into a long throw automatically. The athlete first needs to do the right thing with that position. Did they actively accelerate the hammer? Or were they just passive? Even though the positions are similar, accelerating the hammer will help the throw while being passive won't.

Analyzing the movements shifts the focus from quantity to quality. Moving the hammer correctly can often make up for poor positions. Thankfully, we do not have to settle for one or the other. Improvements in one often lead to improvements in the other: better positions make it easier to move and good movements make it easier to keep strong positions. The right coach can find both the right positions and the movements, the quantity and the quality.

• • •

The Coaching. After you analyze an athlete's positions and movements and understand what aspects he or she should improve, the final step is to figure out how to actually change the technique. This is where good coaches, who can identify problems, are distinguished from great coaches, who can fix them.

Sometimes fixing the problem is as simple as saying what you want, but most of the time it is more complex. For starters, each athlete learns somewhat differently. What works for one may not work for another. You have to find the cue that the athlete best responds to, and that cue is often changing as the athlete becomes more or less responsive to the same inputs. Next, you may have to focus on one part of the throw to fix a completely different part. Deconstructing the chain of problems can be endless, and you may be adjusting the head position in order to realign the foot. This is where coaching meets art. Experience will help, but a willingness to think outside the box is paramount.

• • •

The following chapters will first take a more detailed look at the science of hammer throwing and my underlying philosophy of the event before going into more detail about each of these three levels.

5 // THE BASIC SCIENCE OF HAMMER THROWING

As I discussed in the Introduction, my philosophy of hammer throwing is speed. The event may look and sound complex, but in the end the success or failure of each throw comes down to how fast the hammer is going. The faster the hammer is traveling when it is released, the farther it will fly.

• • •

Speed is certainly not the only element affecting the hammer, but there is a reason I single it out: it is, by far, the most important element. Along with the angle and height of release, speed belongs to the core group of three factors that are actually under the thrower's control. However, the other two elements do not show anywhere near the same impact on results that speed does. Past biomechanical studies have shown an increase in speed of around one meter per second can add five meters to a throw.[6] On the other hand, releasing the hammer a few centimeters higher off the ground will add only a few inches to the distance. Optimizing the degree of release by as much as five degrees translates to around one meter of distance.[7]

In addition to the three controllable factors, there are many environmental factors—such as the air resistance due to air temperature, density,

THE BALL & CHAIN

TABLE 2: 2009 WORLD CHAMPIONSHIPS ANALYSIS				
Thrower	Distance	Speed of Release (rank)	Angle of Release (rank)	Final Turn Speed (rank)
Kozmus	80.84	28.2 m/s (1)	42.6° (2)	0.48 s (1)
Ziolkowski	78.09	27.7 m/s (2)	40.8° (4)	0.52 s (5)
Pars	77.45	27.5 m/s (3)	44.5° (1)	0.52 s (5)
Esser	76.27	27.5 m/s (3)	39.9° (6)	0.52 s (5)
Haklits	76.26	27.4 m/s (5)	41.4° (3)	0.50 s (2)
Litvinov Jr.	76.00	27.4 m/s (5)	39.9° (6)	0.50 s (2)
Kryvitski	76.00	27.3 m/s (7)	40.2° (5)	0.50 s (2)

wind, altitude, and a plethora of other factors. These environmental factors often have a larger effect on distance than the elements under an athlete's control. As I stated earlier, changes in the angle of release or height of release usually add only centimeters to a throw, but studies have shown that a strong tailwind of eight meters per second can add two meters to a world class throw.[8] A competition venue with an altitude of 1,000 meters can add a half meter when compared to sea level.[9] However, these distances can be dwarfed by the negative effect brought on by a heavy downpour of rain during a meet.

After looking at all the factors, both controlled and environmental, it becomes even clearer that speed plays the greatest role. The environmental elements can be significant, but cannot be controlled. The other controllable factors offer control but little significance. There is just one factor under the athlete's control that has a big impact. That element is speed.

• • •

Speed can be a deceptive term. The speed I am referring to, and the speed that biomechanists have referenced, is not the speed of the hammer thrower. The speed that matters is the speed of the hammer. Both are important since all elite hammer throwers move both their bodies and the hammer fast. Furthermore a fast body can help a fast hammer. But despite this connection is still a big difference between them. At the end of the throw, the hammer is the thing being released into the field. Therefore, its speed and not the thrower's speed determines how far it goes.

The data compiled at the German Olympic Training Center in Hessen, shown in Table 2, comes from seven four-turn throwers at the 2009 World Championships.[10] Three of the throwers that completed their final turn the fastest also had the lowest result of the group. How quick the turn was completed is a measure of body speed, but body speed is just one factor in creating hammer speed. Body speed must also be transferred to the hammer. The transferences come down to science.

The longer an athlete's radius, the more their speed is amplified or translated into the speed of the hammer. A shorter radius can reduce the hammer's speed. In comparing these results to similar analyses done at other competitions, athletes like Krisztián Pars have actually thrown farther with a slower final turn. In these cases Pars had a slightly longer radius that allowed more speed to transfer to the hammer despite slower body movements. Sometimes additional body speed comes at the sacrifice of stability, which also prevents an athlete from having a strong powerful release that can transfer even more energy to the hammer.

The data from the 2009 World Championships also allows a chance to look at the other controllable factors. All things being equal, you can see that a steeper angle of release is better. However, adding several degrees to the throw contributed only centimeters to the distance for many throwers. Ranking the athletes by their angle of release in no way correlates to the actual results of the athletes. The only time it played a role was when two athletes had the same or close to the same hammer velocity; in that case the steeper orbit resulted in a better throw. For example, it served as a tie breaker between Pars and Esser and between Haklits and Litvinov.

Because the height of release plays even less of a role, it was not docu-

THE BALL & CHAIN

mented in the study of the 2009 World Championships. The ideal release is at shoulder height, which is effectively fixed for each athlete. If an athlete tries to release higher, any benefit is greatly outweighed by a loss of speed. The movement required to achieve the higher release is not ideal for accelerating the hammer, thus resulting in a loss of speed.

The speed of the hammer, on the other hand, provides a nearly perfect prediction of the final results. Ranking the athletes by speed shows the same results as ranking them by distance. Therefore, once again, speed is king.

• • •

I mentioned radius in passing in the last section. It requires a more detailed discussion since it is one of the more important concepts in the hammer throw and a key element in generating speed. A longer radius can increase hammer speed, without any acceleration on the part of the athlete, by forcing the hammer to travel a longer path in the same amount of time.

To explain this concept, let's take a step back to geometry class and look at the example of a wheel. Imagine a wheel rotating at a constant speed of one revolution per second. If the spoke of the wheel is one meter long, the wheel will travel 6.28 meters in one second. The distance traveled is simply equal to the circumference of the wheel (pi multiplied by the diameter of the wheel). If the spoke is extended to 1.5 meters, the circumference of the wheel also increases, resulting in a larger distance travelled of 9.42 meters per rotation. Therefore, even if the rotation speed is kept at a constant one revolution per second, the speed of the wheel can increase from 22.6 kilometers per hour to 33.9 kilometers per hour simply by making the spokes longer.

In the hammer throw, the athlete is the center of the wheel, his or her arms are the spokes, and the hammer follows the path of the tire. The parts are different but the same principles apply. You don't have to accelerate the body to accelerate the hammer. Lengthening the radius will increase the hammer speed because the hammer has to go faster to keep up with the body.

∙ ∙ ∙

Understanding and analyzing data like this is quite easy. But this is just the first step in the process. Making the data useful in training is much more difficult since data only measures the effects of a throw, not the causes. Finding a cause is a long process that often involves counterintuitive changes like slowing down to maintain radius, as we saw above. This transfer from science and theory to practice requires a coach, not just a biomechanist.

Nevertheless, the coach still needs the data. Data provides valuable feedback that can help in technical analysis and goal setting. You can try to get stronger, get bigger, and improve your technique. All of these things can help you throw far. But they all help via the same route: they help you move the ball faster. A thorough understanding of the basic science of hammer throwing is therefore needed for coaches of all experience levels to determine how each technical change can help improve the speed of the hammer. As the next three chapters take a deeper look at the three levels of technique, continue to think about how each aspect of the technique helps the ball move faster.

6 // THE POSITIONS

Coaching technique begins with looking at an athlete's positions. Before I begin a discussion on positions, I have to put out a disclaimer. Perhaps it is the lawyer in me, but I need to warn you that discussing positions is a dangerous task unless they are considered in context.

Technique in the hammer throw is not just about mastering positions, it is about mastering forces. What position an athlete is in is often dictated by what forces he or she needs to react to or generate. By nature, all athletes are different. They vary in many ways including size, shape, strengths, and weaknesses. All of these variations affect the forces at play in the throw and, as a result, affect how the athlete must adapt and what positions they will need to be in.

For example, two of the most successful athletes in the Soviet Union were world record holders Yuriy Sedykh and Jüri Tamm. Combined, they won five Olympic medals, and likely would have won two more if not for the 1984 Olympic boycott.

Sedykh and Tamm were very different athletes; Tamm was a larger, stronger athlete while Sedkyh was fast and precise. They shared a coach, but their technique varied quite a bit. Yet both were able to attain substantial success despite their technical differences. Their individual style was suited to let them master the different forces generated through their personal characteristics and style. Former Australian national pole vault coach Alan Launder explains this point well when discussing vaulters:

> The critical point here is that while the similarities in the techniques of these athletes are determined by biomechanical imperatives, the differences are determined by each athlete's unique characteristics. So an athlete's style overlays their technical model which should be based on the principles of biomechanics.[11]

Even when the positions are the same, focusing on them rather than on the forces can be a mistake. One of the first hammer clinics I attended featured a coach going into immense detail about many small facets of the throw. He discussed the ideal time at which the foot should lift off the ground, the proper angle of the ankle, and some other small details concerning footwork. In the years since, I have never really thought about these points during my throw. My foot is pulled off the ground by the force of rotation and not by a volitional act.

If a thrower masters the forces in the throw, the body will find the right positions. If Sedykh or Tamm's technique was instead focused on reaching exact positions, both might not have been able to handle the immense forces created in their throws.

In this chapter, I break down the hammer throw into its constituent parts, and doing this can naturally lead the reader to also focus on the small details and positions in the throw. This misses the big picture. The reason I am still undergoing this task is twofold. First, while learning the throw as a whole is helpful, a coach eventually needs to understand the parts. Second, positions often show effects and might not be the best focus for fixing problems, but they can be useful tools in diagnosing problems. Consider yourself warned.

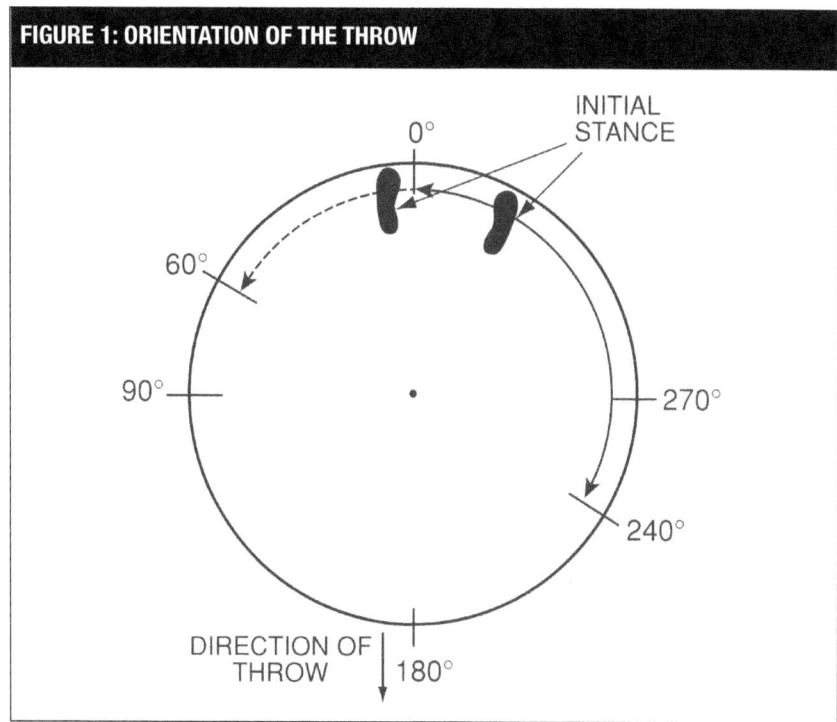

FIGURE 1: ORIENTATION OF THE THROW

In talking about technique in general, it is also helpful to have a common language. Figure 1 illustrates the different terminology that will be used throughout the remainder of this book regarding the position of the body or hammer during the throw in relation to the outside world. This is a useful and commonly referenced guide for positions.

In addition, I will often refer to the terms single or double support. These terms refer to the phases in the throw where, respectively, either one or both feet are in contact with the ground.

To simplify matters I will also discuss technique only as it would apply to a right-handed thrower turning counter-clockwise. The same comments can also be applied to a left-handed thrower in reverse.

FIGURE 2: THE WINDS - POSITIONS 1 TO 10

• • •

The Winds. The vast majority of the speed generated during the throw is generated during the preliminary winds. Therefore, the winds are the thrower's best chance to set the speed and rhythm of the throw. Figure 2 illustrates the preliminary winds. The fixed horizontal and vertical lines in each position mark the highest point of the thrower's head and the center (turning axis) of the orbiting hammer.

Several technical points can be observed in the winds. First, the body stays fairly balanced without too much shifting of weight from side to side. Naturally the body will move a little in order to oppose the moving forces of the hammer, but the feet and hips should remain aligned towards the back of the ring, and the thrower should feel in control and relaxed throughout these movements. The whole body should be centered with just slightly more weight over the left side, as shown in positions 3 and 4. The left side will be the turning axis throughout the throw, so it is important to set up a proper axis by loading the left leg with a slightly larger percentage of the body weight.

Second, the winds are the only time the arms should be bent during the throw. After pushing the hammer across the front to gain some initial speed, the arms will then bend as the hammer passes over the top of the athlete's head. To initiate this movement, the athlete can think of rolling the right hand over the left hand and then pulling the right hand towards the center point of his or her head while keeping the left forearm within millimeters of the right cheek as shown in positions 3 and 4.

Third, once the hammer moves back behind the head, the athlete needs to turn his/her shoulders to create a little torque between the shoulders and the hips, which are still oriented towards 0° as shown in position 6. The shoulders should remain relatively level throughout this process. From this position, the athlete can straighten the arms and push or sweep the hammer out away and across the front of the body, using this torque. The low point should be between the two feet, and the shoulder axis should catch up with the hip axis by this point, as shown in position 7.

Finally, this process is repeated during the second wind, but with a faster tempo. Most elite throwers use just two winds, while a few also include a third wind.

• • •

The Entry. After the last wind, the thrower will begin the entry into the first turn. Before discussing the entry, it is helpful to note that there are two main varieties of technique for the first turn which affect how the entry is typed. A majority of the world's current elite throwers use four turns in the throw and complete the first turn entirely on the ball of their foot in what is known as a "toe-turn." This can be necessary in order to fit four turns into the ring since it requires less space than the standard "heel-toe" turn. For the purposes of this discussion, I will focus on the heel-toe turn.

Whether or not a toe-turn might be the best long-term fit for an athlete, it is essential to learn a proper heel-toe turn first since it simplifies the throw and perfects the movement that is used on every thrower's final

THE BALL & CHAIN

three turns. Furthermore, the current men's world record was set with just three heel-toe turns, so it may end up being the optimal technique for an athlete anyway.

The entry into the first turn begins before the last wind has even finished. As the hammer descends in the last wind, the thrower's body will begin to lower slightly and sit back against the pull of the hammer. The arms will be fully extended as they continue to accelerate the hammer through the low point. As opposed to the winds, throwers will, at this point, often have concave shoulders to extend the radius of the hammer as it reaches its low point. The back also remains erect at this point, as shown in positions 12 through 14 of Figure 3.

Once the hammer reaches its low point, the thrower's head, shoulders, hands, and hammer should all be oriented in the same direction, as shown in position 12. While the head is oriented in the direction of the hammer, the athlete should not be looking down at the hammer. The eyes should be focused on the horizon above the hammer and should remain looking slightly above the hammer throughout the throw. This orientation should be locked in throughout the throw. While the hips might move slightly ahead or behind, the rest of the body including the head, shoulders, hands, and hammer should continue to be aligned until the release.

After the hammer reaches the low point, the thrower should continue to push the hammer to the left to create the optimal radius. Rather than

FIGURE 3: THE WINDS - POSITIONS 11 TO 14

Hammer Throw Technique

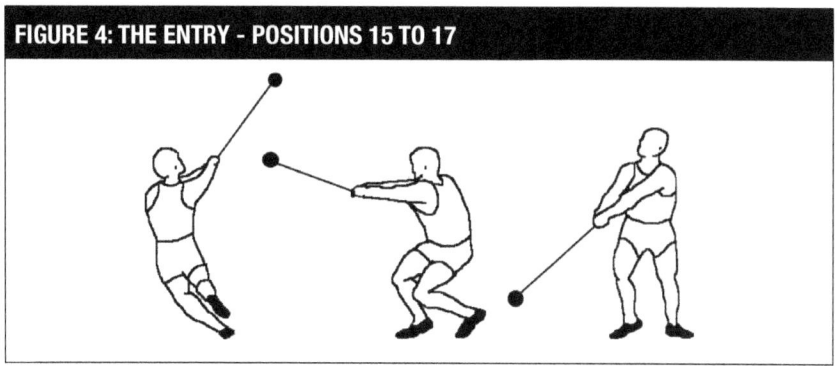

FIGURE 4: THE ENTRY - POSITIONS 15 TO 17

thinking about pushing the hammer steeply up, the thrower should think about pushing the hammer around. With speed, the hammer will rise naturally without active effort by the thrower to make it steeper. At the same time, the ball of the right foot and the heel of the left foot rotate in unison.

The right foot should attempt to remain in contact with the ground until the hammer feels like it has passed 90 degrees. In actuality, the forces of the hammer will often pull it off the ground sooner.

• • •

The First Turn. Once the right foot has left the ground, the athlete has entered the single support phase. Unlike other throwing events, there is no "flight" phase and the hammer thrower should always maintain contact with the ground through the left foot. The right foot, however, will alternate phases of ground contact.

During the single support phase the knees and legs should stay close together. As the right foot leaves the ground, it should actively step over the left ankle, as shown in position 15 of Figure 4. This movement reduces the duration of the single support phase and also allows the hip axis to slightly overtake the shoulder axis and once again create torque, as shown in position 16.

As the right foot lands, the body should again counter back slightly to-

THE BALL & CHAIN

FIGURE 5: THE FIRST TURN - POSITIONS 18 TO 26

wards the left side to maintain a stable axis of rotation. The hips are also at their lowest height of the turn in order to counter the force of the hammer as it reaches its highest point. The thrower should then, again, actively push the hammer down to the low point while simultaneously countering the increasing speed of the hammer.

• • •

Subsequent Turns. Once the hammer again reaches the low point, the same process is repeated throughout the remaining turns. The thrower must push the hammer far out again to the left so that the hammer nearly leads the thrower through the turn, rather than the thrower's legs or the left shoulder leading the system. This dynamic is illustrated in positions 18 and 19 of Figure 5.

After the next single support phase ends, the arms should remain straight, continuing to form an isosceles triangle. The thrower simultaneously drops with a bent left knee as the right foot touches the ground, all while maintaining a strong left axis as shown in position 21. By pushing the hammer to the low point again, with relaxed arms and concave shoulders, the thrower

returns to a stable, centered position, as shown in positions 22 and 23.
The following turn should be executed in exactly the same manner except that as the speed of the hammer increases, the thrower's body will simultaneously lean back slightly more in order to counter the increased force of the implement. For example, notice the slight difference between positions 20 and 26.

• • •

The Release. The release begins once the right foot lands on the final turn. The immediate response should be the same as with the other turns: continue to accelerate the hammer with a long motion to the left. The mindset of the thrower throughout the release should also be as if they are entering another turn. If a thrower instead focuses on the release he or she may inadvertently pull with the left shoulder, thus decreasing the hammer's radius and speed and, therefore, the distance of the throw.

Instead the thrower should continue to push the hammer and maintain a long radius all the way to 90 degrees. The legs will straighten and the hips will come forward as the head tilts back to counter the hammer as its forces reach the highest point in the throw. Upon release, the head of most throwers is so far back that it is in fact looking skyward. All this is done while maintaining the same vertical axis over the left foot as shown in positions 28 through 30 of Figure 6. Finally, the hands then release the hammer and continue up into the air, as shown in position 31.

FIGURE 6: THE RELEASE - POSITIONS 27 TO 31

THE BALL & CHAIN

・・・

With a basic understanding of the parts and positions of the throw, it is time to quickly move towards a more important element: connecting the positions together with the right movements.

7 // THE MOVEMENTS

Analyzing positions is often done by reviewing the throw frame-by-frame. Looking at the movements, on the other hand, requires you to press the play button, sit back, and just watch. As I said earlier, technique in the hammer throw is not about mastering positions, it is about mastering forces. The positions allow you to diagnose problems, but the movements are the way to actually manipulate the forces in the throw. After all, a position alone does not create speed. Speed is generated by what you do with that position.

• • •

The most important aspect of the movements is rhythm. Every throw has a rhythm, as does each component of the throw. Each turn has a rhythm of acceleration. The asynchronous movements of the body and the hammer have a rhythm. Even the sound of the throw has a rhythm to it. It is hard to describe the rhythm of a good throw, but Figure 7 at least visualizes it better than words can.[12] The rhythm of the acceleration and deceleration build until the throw is released.

Hammer throwers fall into three main categories of overall rhythm in the throw. The first group begins slowly with a drastic increase in speed during each turn. The second group is the opposite: they begin with a lot of speed already in the winds but then have very minimal acceleration during the turns. A final group begins with average speed and moderate acceleration in each turn.

No single approach is better than the other. What is important about the rhythm is that it is there and fits the individual. As Bondarchuk once told me, "The difference in structure of the rhythm doesn't prevent an athlete from showing a high level of athletic achievement, but to the contrary it facilitates it." A coach must identify which rhythm is natural to the athlete and cultivate that. This will allow the athlete to best accelerate the hammer throughout the throw.

• • •

Once an athlete's rhythm is found, it is important to focus on it in training. It is difficult to transfer technical improvements made with one rhythm to another rhythm. For example, an athlete of the fast-starting variety may be able to improve a technical problem while doing slow-turning drills. However, the dynamic of their normal throws varies so much that it is unlikely that doing slow drills will also completely solve the problem in their normal throw. Therefore, it is important to also train at an athlete's normal rhythm in order to ensure the technical improvements carry over into that rhythm and hold up under the stress and force of a normal throw.

• • •

While the rhythm represents the movement of the whole system, the orbit represents the movement of the hammer itself. Like the orbit of the moon rotating around the Earth, the orbit of the hammer is its path around the thrower.

The most discussed part of the orbit is the low point, with coaches often talking about if it should be to the left or to the right (i.e., before or after 0 degrees). But focusing on the low point is just focusing on a two-dimensional snapshot of the orbit. In addition to being left or right, the hammer can be too high or too low. And the most important aspect is yet another dimension: time. Where the hammer was and where the hammer is going is just as important as where it is. Orbit is therefore quite complex. To simplify it, I like to focus on four points that can easily improve the orbit.

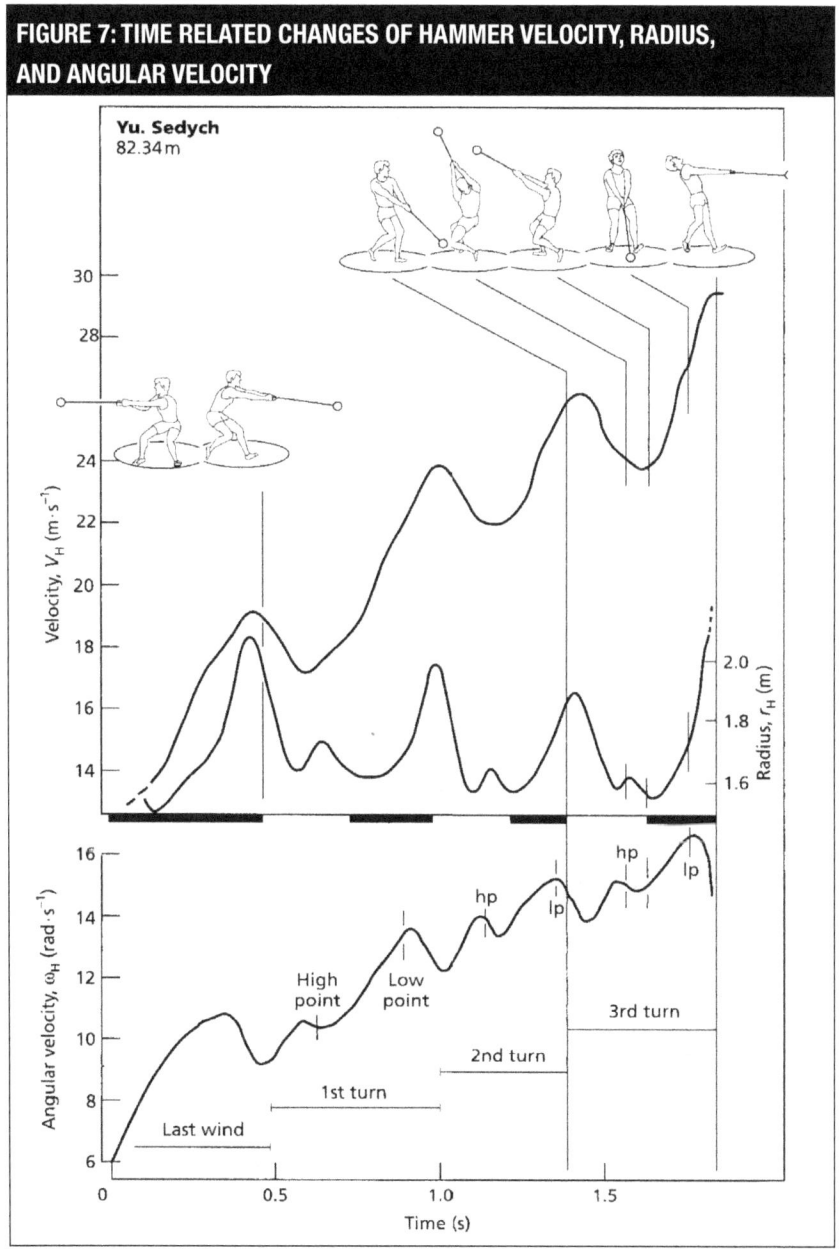

FIGURE 7: TIME RELATED CHANGES OF HAMMER VELOCITY, RADIUS, AND ANGULAR VELOCITY

THE BALL & CHAIN

Big Circles. Orbit is closely connected to rhythm and rhythm requires fluidity. The more you jerk the hammer around, the more you will disrupt its momentum. Ideally, you want to make big circles with the hammer. The middle of this circle is the thrower's left side, which serves as the axis of rotation. For example, take a look at an overhead view of 1997 World Champion Heinz Weis's orbit in Figure 8 and you will see what I'm talking about.[13] If you compare this with someone who drags the hammer, the circles would not be nearly as circular, and each circle would be progressively smaller. If your axis shifts to the right side, you also start making some weird shapes.

Long Path. As described in Chapter 5, long throws come from increasing the speed of the hammer. The thrower can accelerate the hammer while going the same speed by increasing the system's radius, i.e. the distance between the thrower and the ball. A longer radius means the hammer will make a bigger circle. And if the hammer has to travel a longer distance in the same amount of time, it will be moving faster.

Checkpoints. I first started to understand the orbit when I visited Olympic Champion Sergey Litvinov for a training camp a decade ago. Rather than talking about the low point, he told me to focus on hitting consistent checkpoints to the left and right of the low point at 45 degrees and 315 degrees. If I focused on making sure the hammer traveled through these imaginary checkpoints, then it would create not only a good low point but also the correct orbit throughout the throw. After all, a thrower can have a perfect low point and terrible orbit at the same time if the orbit is tilted, too steep, or too small. But if the thrower focuses more on the path of the hammer, then a good orbit quickly follows.

Relinquish Control. As I said earlier, a thrower shouldn't jerk the hammer around. Instead, let the hammer's momentum control the throw by turning the athlete. The hammer is an inanimate object, but it knows what to do as long as it has an axis to turn around. Stay centered during the throw, and it will do the work. Here is an experiment Connolly taught me.

Attach a string with a weight at the end of it to the top of a pencil. Now hold it vertically and start swinging the weight around. Immediately, you will notice that the more weird movements you make to increase the speed actually cause the weight to lose momentum. If you keep the pencil moving around a stable axis, the weight will move and even accelerate with very little effort of your own. The same is true with the hammer.

FIGURE 8: REFERENCE DEGREE & TIME CHART FOR MOVEMENT ANALYSIS, INCORPORATING ORBIT OF THE HAMMER
[(a) side view and (b) overhead view]

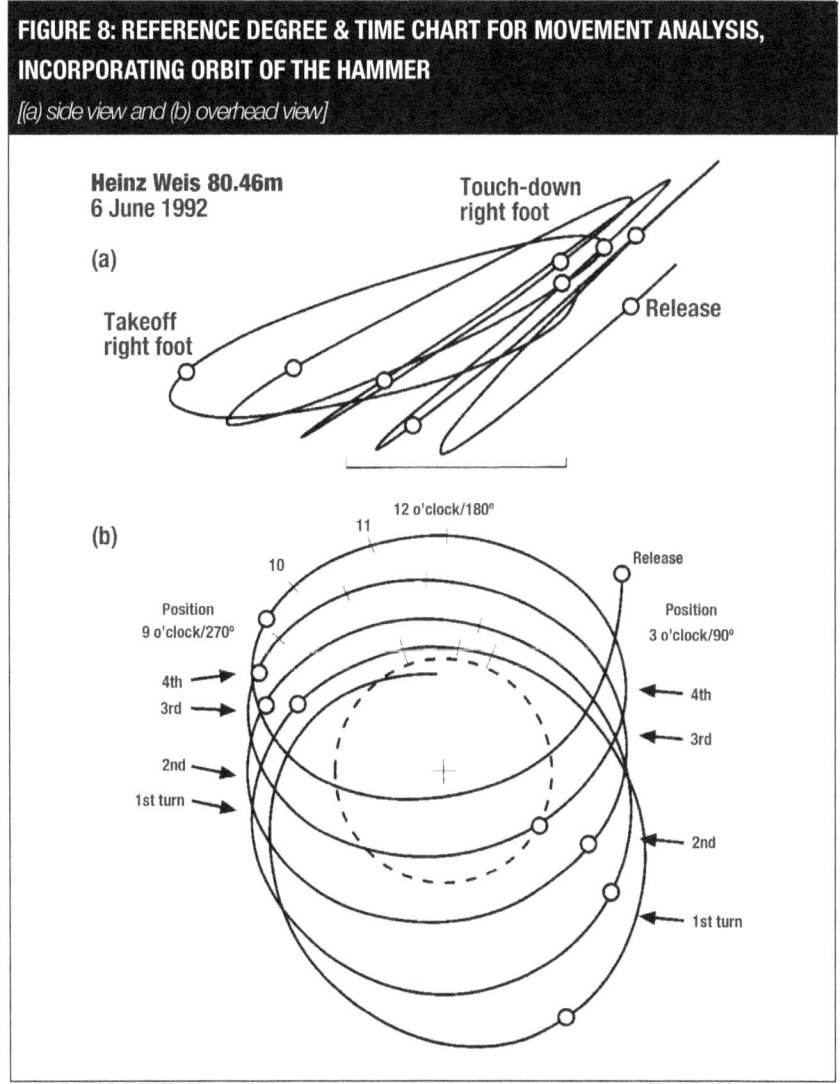

THE BALL & CHAIN

• • •

Only through adding the correct movements to the correct positions can a thrower get the most out of a throw. Alas, as with most things in life, it is easier said than done. Knowing what to do and knowing how to do it are very different concepts. What bridges the gap is good coaching that can direct the athlete on how to reach the right positions and movements in his/her throw.

8 // COACHING

The way a coach expresses their analysis of positions and movements is where their role turns from science to art. Harry Marra, the coach of world decathlon record holder Ashton Eaton, visited me in 2013 and explained this in two words: Elton John. Just before we met, World Championships heptathlon silver medalist Brianne Theisen-Eaton made a breakthrough in the javelin. When we began discussing javelin technique, he said the key for him was Elton John.

Coaching comes down to communication. At the beginning, the coach must know what the athlete should do. At the end, the goal is that the athlete will accomplish the task at hand. The bridge between the two is communication. Proper communication gets the athlete to do what is needed.

The tricky part about communication is that it is so personal. Each individual coach must find a way to communicate with each individual athlete. Finding the best way to communicate can be difficult, resulting in methods than bear only a passing resemblance to the original message. This is where Elton John comes in. Marra used the name Elton John as a cue to transform Theisen-Eaton's technique. As he explained it to me:

> Elton John is a great piano player and vocalist. Piano playing skills are gross in nature relative to moving up

and down the keyboard with your arms. The fingers on each hand are finite skills. The javelin is very similar. Many parts of the throw are a gross skill, like the violent pull with the arm/shoulder, the violent drive/turn of the right hip during the delivery phase, the aggressive explosion of legs at delivery, etc. But it also has finite skills.

If all of the above are done correctly, but the javelin itself is not placed correctly and firmly in the hand (finger dexterity) and kept there throughout this entire delivery phase, all of these gross skills are for naught and may lead to an injury. Hence, the Elton John cue means remember to keep finger control on the jav during the approach and delivery phase so every aspect line up correctly.[14]

Note how long that explanation was. As Marra noted later, he can't give that sermon to an athlete after each throw. But after months of practice and understanding each other, all of a sudden he can replace that explanation with just two words, "Elton John," and his athlete will know what he means.

Analyzing the positions or movements in a throw can be done by a biomechanist as well as by a coach. With proper programming, a computer might even be able to accomplish this task in the future. No matter who does such an analysis, it can be helpful in setting technical goals and assessing whether they have been reached or not. But the analysis does not tell the coach how to reach the goal. That requires communication. This chapter discusses how coaches communicate with athletes and explains some situations where the best communication path may not be the obvious one.

• • •

Fixing a technical problem starts with a cue. Cues are the language of coaching. They are the instructions or tips given to an athlete in order to try and fix a problem. Just as finding the right words can separate a good writer from a bad writer, finding the right cue separates good coaches from other coaches.

The first step in finding a cue is to understand the difference between what you are trying to accomplish and how you want to accomplish it. This is the difference between cause and effect. In some cases, the cause and effect are so closely linked that they are practically the same thing. More often than not, however, it is a problem earlier in the throw that manifests itself as an issue later in the throw.

For example, let's take a thrower with an unstable release. For such an athlete, "stabilize the release" is not a helpful cue since this just restates the problem. A better way to fix the problem might be to focus on the root cause of the problem at the start of the throw and instruct a thrower to focus on a point which can lead to a more stable release such as, "keep a longer double support phase on the entry."

∙ ∙ ∙

Once you understand the difference between cause and effect, you then need to find which cue will help the most. This is highly individual as athletes learn in different ways and respond differently to the same input. The German and Russian approaches to teaching technique vary significantly but both try to maximize the same technical goals. The difference is that they use vastly different cues to get there. Neither may be right or wrong, they are just different paths to throwing far. Simply put, what works for me may not work for you.

Finding the right cue for each thrower is often a process of trial and error. Unless you try different things, you may not ever find the cues that work for you. After you accumulate some cues that work, you can start to get an idea of how the athletes learn, and that will be helpful in finding other cues that might work. Below are some ideas that can help you experiment and find tools like cues that you may not have otherwise thought of by using overemphasis, shifting the focus, and even paradoxes.

THE BALL & CHAIN

• • •

Overemphasis. Another key concept to understand is the difference between what you think and what you do. A coach may use a cue that does not relate to the technical goals, but the body may react correctly because the cue points the right direction. I've had a few heated exchanges with one coach over this exact concept. He was critical of Yuriy Sedykh because Sedykh's advice about throwing did not match measurements of his own throws. He stated at a clinic that he never tried to lower his center of gravity during the throw, contrary to several studies which clearly showed that his hips dropped 30 centimeters (one foot) in his final turn. To complicate things further, Sedykh was telling athletes to try and keep double support until 110 degrees in the first turn, when video showed his left foot clearly left the ground before 55 degrees.

For me, Sedykh's cue made sense even if it didn't conform to any scientific measurements of his own throw. Ideally the foot should come off the ground when the forces of the hammer require it. If Sedykh thought about lifting the foot off the ground at 55 degrees, he may have anticipated it and lifted his foot off earlier than this natural moment. When he instead thought about a later point, a point which was likely impossible for him to reach, it let the hammer have control again and thus allowed the right foot to come off at a natural point that maintained balance better. While I cannot be sure, perhaps that is what Sedykh was trying to do. In any event, it worked as a tool for helping me and my athletes improve our technique.

• • •

Changing the Focus. Sometimes you want a cue to focus on something further up the causal chain and other times you need to shift the focus solely because it is not possible or practical to directly address the problem. As with overemphasis, this can also be counterintuitive.

A good example of this comes from the world of sprinting. Sprinting is predominantly a lower-body-dominant movement, but the legendary and infamous sprint coach Charlie Francis didn't focus on the legs in order to get a powerful start out of the blocks. In his autobiography, he laid out some of the facts facing a sprinter at the start of the race, as he learned from his mentor Harry Jerome:

> [W]hen a sprinter tries to accelerate, he must be patient above all. There are two variables to consider: time warp within a sprinter's mind, where each second drags like ten; and the fact that it takes a moment for your body to transmit your acceleration onto the track.[15]

While the legs are doing much of the work, the situation, as he describes it, makes it difficult to use them in instructions to the athlete. Such a cue may actually hinder acceleration by reducing the athlete's patience. As Francis told it, both Jerome and another mentor, Percy Duncan, therefore advised a different focus, "'If you concentrated on your arms and your hand position,' they told me, 'your feet would automatically land in the right spots.'"

Many coaches, myself included, often use a similar approach in the hammer. The delay in time between thinking about doing something and it actually happening also occurs in the hammer. By thinking about lower body cues, patience can be destroyed. However if you focus on the pushing of the hammer with the upper body, the footwork will take care of itself just as it did for the sprinters. This illustrates just one instance where it may be helpful to focus on something completely different than what you are trying to fix.

• • •

Paradoxes. So far, my discussion of technique has stayed within the bounds of logic. But in coaching, things can often depart that realm. Sometimes fixing technique can be a paradox. Bondarchuk once told me about a former hammer thrower of his that had a bad habit of having a high point that was both too high and too early in the first turn. For four years, Bondarchuk would tell him to flatten out the orbit and the athlete

THE BALL & CHAIN

only made marginal success on that point. Finally, as the athlete was about to finish his university degree and move to another city, Bondarchuk had run out of ideas and told him to just make his orbit even steeper. To everyone's surprise, the throw actually flattened out. Bondarchuk had told him to emphasize everything wrong about the throw, and he ended up doing everything right.

Bondarchuk isn't the only coach to try this method. When I was in high school, I read an article by former nationally-ranked hammer thrower Greg Gassner about paradoxes in the hammer throw, and it has stuck with me ever since. Gassner noted that hammer throwers are often required to do opposite things at the same time: such as relaxing while applying force or giving to the hammer to create radius while sitting back to counter the implement. He continued:

> The hammer throw, as described here, is paradoxical in nature. Why not use paradoxical intervention to teach these concepts. Paradoxical intervention is a concept borrowed from family therapists ... The basic premise is to "prescribe the symptom"; that is, ask the athlete to do just what he has been so consciously trying to avoid! ... For instance, if an athlete is resisting your attempts to get him to extend his arms, then anticipate his resistance by telling him to do the opposite, that is to bend his arms.[16]

I mention this because I have tried a similar approach in my own training, at times. One of my technical flaws is that I often do not have enough weight on my left side during the start of the throw because I turn my left foot and hip too early, thus pushing my weight over to the right side. My initial approach to fix this problem was to be more patient with the left foot so that it did not turn early, but this only helped marginally. The next time, I tried the opposite: to be more active with the feet. While this did not immediately fix the problem, it surprised me by helping substantially. Thinking about paradoxes can be another tool to use when all else fails.

• • •

The process of coaching technique does not end once you find the correct cue for the right athlete. Just as the effectiveness of a new exercise diminishes once the body gets used to it, the effectiveness of a technical cue also wears off. I call this cue staleness. After focusing on one technical point in the same way for a month, it is often time to try a new approach. You can always come back to the old approach, and it will likely work again with renewed freshness, but you have to keep changing if you want to make progress. You have to keep the body from reaching a comfort zone. One way to do that is to frequently try new cues with the same goal in mind.

• • •

Cue staleness also must be balanced with cue overload. As with other aspects of training, too much change can be just as bad as too little change. Each technical change and each cue first requires time for the athlete to adapt to it and then requires additional time for it to enter the athlete's muscle memory. Only after this point can the athlete execute the new movement without consciously focusing on it during each throw. If a coach continues to add cues before prior problems have been solved, the athlete will likely be overwhelmed and unable to make progress on any of the technical points. As a rule of thumb, I find it difficult for most athletes to focus on more than one or two technical points per session.

Because of this limitation, prioritizing is important. Coaches must focus on the most important technical problems first before moving on to less important points. There is no sense in wasting valuable training time focusing on a small point when a larger point looms. In some cases, fixing the bigger problems will also inadvertently fix the smaller problems. In all cases, each cue should be clear and given a chance to become stale before it is changed.

• • •

What makes this sport fun is that each coach must develop their own path for their own athletes. In this way, coaching approaches an art form where coaches must choose to be creative in identifying a solution to the

THE BALL & CHAIN

problems at hand. And just as we want our athletes to continuously improve, coaches must also continuously seek ways to find new approaches to old problems, identify new problems, and still keep the process simple, straightforward, and easy for athlete to implement.

PART III //

ADVANCED TECHNIQUE

9 // COMMON PROBLEMS AND SOLUTIONS

No matter how erratic a thrower's technique may be, a coach can already begin the process of refining it once the athlete can simply execute a three-turn throw. Using the steps laid out in Chapter 3, getting to this point and building the technical foundation is a quick process. In an analogy to pottery, the athlete has now been formed into the basic geometric shape of the object. The coach, like the potter, can now begin to turn the shape into art by making subtle changes.

The first step in refining technique is to understand the positions, movements, and coaching needed to make improvements. These points were discussed in the last part. The next step is putting them all together. As discussed in the last chapter, knowing what to do and knowing how to do it are very different concepts. This chapter passes along recommendations that will help coaches identify errors in a throw and begin working with the thrower to fix them.

Also mentioned in the last part were two points on coaching that bear repeating as we dive into ways to refine technique. First, the process of improving technique can be very individual. Verbal coaching cues that work for one thrower may not work for another, even if the problem is the same. Second, it is important to remember that the refining process is done at the same rhythm of the throw. A thrower best learns the technical positions—and how to apply them with rhythm during the throw—through repeated throwing rather than drills. This becomes more relevant as a thrower reaches higher levels of performance. Think back on these points as we proceed through problems in the various parts of the throw.

• • •

The Winds and Entry. The start of the throw is in many ways the heart of the throw itself. A good start means a good throw just as a bad start can mean a bad throw because success and failure at the start of the throw is amplified in each subsequent turn. If you make a big mistake at the start, it is nearly impossible to overcome. But, by setting up a throw with the proper balance and rhythm, the rest of the throw can fall into place with minimal effort.

The one positive aspect of problems at the start of the throw is it can be easier to consciously focus on these compared to problems later in the throw. As a coach, it is sometimes enough to simply restate such problems to the athlete and tell him/her not to do it anymore. However, determining what elements of the winds and entry are the problem is not always easy because the effects normally manifest only in the later turns.

One place to start is with the two common problems areas at the start of the throw: balance and rhythm.

In order to keep a good orbit during the throw, the thrower must be balanced in the center with weight slightly shifted to the left side over the axis of rotation. In order to keep a little more weight over the left foot, it can help to have the thrower lower their left shoulder slightly. Using a starting stance that is either too wide or too narrow can also affect balance, as can excessive swaying back and forth during the winds. Ideally, the feet should be shoulder-width apart. Maintaining good balance in the winds not only provides a strong base to push the hammer, but it also will set up the remaining turns. If balance is affected, it will tilt the axis and orbit, amplifying the problem in each turn. Similarly, a low point that is too far to the right or left will shift the orbit and the balance of the throw. The low point should be between the thrower's feet in front of them or slightly to the right of this point.

As the hammer's speed increases, balance becomes even more important. Here, it helps to remember that while speed is important at the start of the throw, it is the speed of the hammer that matters and not the thrower's speed. Therefore, the thrower's body should remain patient and relaxed. Cues such as "be patient" or "let the ball run" can help the thrower focus on maintaining a patient body while the hammer runs its circular course, all the while maintaining a long radius. Excessive movements forward or backward can also throw off the hammer's orbit. The best position for the thrower is to keep a solid nearly vertical core position throughout the winds and entry. This makes it easy for the hammer to turn around the athlete, as the athlete serves as the central axis.

The rhythm of the winds also generates many problems throughout the rest of the throw. The arms should stay long, straight, and in front of the body, as much as possible. Although they bend during the winds, the athlete should extend the arms quickly when the ball comes around, in front. Waiting too long to extend the arms will mean the thrower has little time to push and accelerate the hammer properly. The shoulders should also be relaxed and rotate with the hammer as it turns around the body. In this way, the rhythm and balance can be fixed together.

Rhythm is also crucial at this point of the throw. A critical mistake for beginners is either not accelerating the hammer or accelerating it too late in the last wind. The thrower should try to accelerate the hammer from 240º until 0º. It is no longer possible to properly accelerate the hammer after it passes the low point since the torque between the shoulder axis and hip axis no longer exists. By pushing the hammer earlier, the hammer gains momentum while the thrower still has both feet on the ground. That momentum will carry the thrower through single support, when the right foot lifts off. To help execute this point, throwers can focus on rotating the shoulders with the hammer, extending the arms earlier, and then, rhythmically adding speed to each wind during this phase.

•••

The First Turn. Patience is again the goal as the hammer passes through the low point and the first turn begins. The three most common problems from 0 degrees to 180 degrees all relate to a lack of patience. Throwers tend to either pull back with the shoulders, pick up the right foot too early, or raise their body's center of gravity as the hammer rises. The first problem cuts off the hammer's orbit and reduces radius. The second throws off balance. The third prevents effective countering of the throw. All three cause major problems later in the final turns, but each can be fixed with patience at the start of the throw.

Correcting the first problem of pulling the shoulders back requires cues that emphasize keeping a long radius and being patient with both the lower and upper body. Rather than trying to control the hammer's path, the thrower should let the hammer continue on its own natural path after it passes through the low point. Attempts to pull it with the upper body, or accelerate prematurely with the lower body will only throw off the hammer's orbit. Helpful cues often focus on telling the athlete the same things that should be a focus in the winds: to let the ball run past the thrower or simply to let the ball run. I have also found it helpful to think about keeping a fixed left side around which the hammer will turn.

A related problem comes when the lower body is too active on the entry. Turning the lower body too early throws off the hammer's orbit since the body is no longer working in unison. In addition, when the lower body begins leading the hammer too much, it becomes more difficult to properly push and accelerate the hammer. Patience helps with this problem too. Rather than thinking of picking the right foot off the ground, throwers can think about keeping contact with the ground and only picking up the foot when the turning momentum pulls the foot off the ground. Ironically, picking up the foot later can also help it land earlier since the body will be better balanced by the time single support starts.

The third problem, rising with the hammer, comes from the fact that patience is not just related to the vertical axis. Throwers also need to be patient with regard to the horizontal axis. After the hammer reaches its low point, it begins to rise, and it can be natural for the thrower to rise with it. However, this is the opposite of what a thrower should be doing. The body should move asynchronously with the hammer in order to counter its force. As the hammer goes up, the body needs to go down. By executing the wrong movements with the legs, the thrower not only loses power, but is then required to counter the force with the upper body by pulling on the hammer in subsequent turns. This creates a slew of additional problems relating to balance, radius, and rhythm. Again, thinking of a fixed left side, staying down, or maintaining a fixed knee bend all help an athlete stop rising during the first turn.

• • •

The Turns. Focusing on technique in the turns is often unnecessary since most technical errors during the turns are the result of errors at the start of the throw. Therefore, fixing the start will usually resolve many issues later in the throw. But, in many cases focusing only on the start does not work, and then, it is necessary to broaden the focus to also include technical points later in the throw. The common problems in the turns relate to rhythm and proper acceleration, or a simple failure to repeat many of the same technical points mentioned above.

Rhythm is an essential part to the entire throw, not just the beginning. Just as a thrower must have the proper rhythm of acceleration in the winds, it must also continue throughout each turn. As a result, the athlete cannot completely relax when the right foot lands each turn. While the arms and shoulders should remain loose, the body must simultaneously accelerate the hammer, sometimes even thinking about it before double support so the body has enough time to react and transfer energy to the hammer. Many throwers visibly stall upon landing, and this pause shifts weight onto the right side, throwing off the hammer's low point and rhythm and preventing the thrower from accelerating the hammer. Proper acceleration and rhythm will help this point.

There is also a fine line between accelerating too little and trying to accelerate too much. Again, it is about rhythm. When throwers try to do too much, it can be counterproductive, since it may cause them to stand up or pull their shoulders in an attempt to accelerate the ball a little more. Both of these moves will instead slow the hammer down. Acceleration should be done with the body and hammer together as a single unit. Compromising the unity in an attempt to accelerate more will only backfire.

Some throwers try to give the right amount of acceleration, but in the wrong way. For example, in an attempt to add radius to the hammer, some throwers pike at the hips by bending forward and sticking their butts out. Again, this movement is counterproductive since it puts the athlete in a position where it is difficult to generate power. Focusing on good posture with a straight back and concave shoulders will help.

The most common remaining technical points to focus on during the turns are often those the athlete is already working on at the start of the throw or during the first wind. Even if an athlete is able to eliminate a problem such as not rising with the hammer, pushing the hammer to the left, or letting the ball run to the left more in the first turn, the problem may arise again in subsequent turns and the athlete should focus on repeating these cues on subsequent turns to completely eliminate the problem.

• • •

The Release. With properly executed winds, entry, and turns, the release is perhaps the easiest phase of the throw.

Biomechanically speaking, the release is also different than the turns.

Slightly more weight is put on the right side and the thrower fully extends the left leg for the first time in the throw, instead of continuing to be patient.

However, from a coaching perspective, the release should be the same as every other turn. This is similar to golf and tennis in some respects. In those sports, the point of contact is not different than the rest of the movement; the athlete has to swing through the ball. In the hammer, the athlete should continue to be balanced and accelerate the hammer in the release, just as in other turns. The main difference is that he or she only needs to let go of the hammer at the appropriate time. If the athlete remains balanced, the release will come naturally. If the athlete is off balance, the error likely began at the start of the throw or is due to the fact that the athlete anticipated the release by pulling the hammer or changing the rhythm slightly.

For example, if the hammer lands outside of the sector to the left side, the cause is most likely that the thrower's path through the circle was wrong. That, in turn, could be caused by a thrower having too much weight over the right side of the body on the first turn instead of transferring the weight to the left side and pushing the hammer out to the left side. Rarely does the problem actually arise in the final turn.

• • •

In the last section I talked about how creativity is needed to solve different technical problems. But a coach needs to prioritize before he or she can be creative. As described in the last chapter, the biggest issues should be addressed first, and only one or two technical points should be dealt with in a training session, so that ample attention and focus is given to each point.

Prioritizing begins by focusing on the start of the throw. More often than not, fixing a problem in the winds and entry, or another major problem at the start of the throw, will fix errors that arise later in the throw. It makes little sense to focus on the small points first since they are often resolved by first fixing the major problems in the throw.

THE BALL & CHAIN

The process of solving technical problems also takes time. Only rarely will an athlete be able to quickly fix a problem. Experienced throwers will take even more time, since their bad habits have been ingrained by tens of thousands of attempts with old technique. Eliminating bad habits can be best accomplished by keeping a narrow focus on just one or two technical points at each training session and continuing with those points until well after they appear corrected. It is difficult for even the world's best throwers to multi-task. By focusing intensely on one item, you are more likely to master it and eventually ingrain the new technique.

10 // BIOMECHANICS

When hammer throwing is viewed with a scientific eye, the thing that jumps out is how important the hammer's speed is in a throw, as explained in Chapter 5. How that speed is generated has occupied teams of biomechanists for the past half century. Rather than getting bogged down in the technical details of each study, this chapter highlights a few of the most relevant and helpful conclusions from the biomechanical analyses of modern technique over the past three decades.

• • •

Single and Double Support. The modern model for hammer throwing technique is based largely on the model developed by the Soviet Union from the 1950s to the 1980s. The theory behind this technique is that the amount of time spent in the double-support phase should be longer than the amount of time spent in the single-support phase. Only through double-support, the theory goes, can an athlete properly accelerate the hammer.

Subsequent studies have analyzed this claim and, for the most part, confirmed the hypothesis. A quick look at the acceleration pattern of the hammer throughout the throw shows that the phases of acceleration overlap very closely with the double support phases and phases of deceleration overlap with the single support phases. For example, the velocity of the hammer throughout world record holder Yuriy Sedykh's throw is shown in Figure 7 in Chapter 7. In this throw the hammer starts and stops accelerating at the same time as double support begins and ends.[17] Sedykh also spent 55.8 percent (55.8%) of the throw in double support, a high percentage of time when compared to his competitors.[18]

A few points should be noted, however. First, the hammer can in fact be accelerated in single support. American biomechanist Jesus Dapena showed that gravity can help accelerate the hammer during the period between when it reaches the high point and when the right foot touches the ground. In addition, the translation of the thrower through the circle can accelerate the hammer.[19] Other biomechanists have observed that there is sometimes acceleration at the start and end of single support, but that this is often ineffective with regards to the overall throw and result only from the angular momentum of pulling the hammer up or down.[20]

It is also interesting that while many elite throwers like Sedykh spent a majority of the throw in double support phase, there were many other elite throwers that spent more time in single support such as 1992 Olympic champion Andrey Abduvaliyev.[21] As helpful as double support is, it is not the only technique that produces good throws.

• • •

Transfer of Energy. Hammer speed doesn't just appear out of nowhere; energy must first be generated by the thrower and then transferred to the hammer. A long double-support phase gives the thrower the best opportunity to accelerate the hammer, but the thrower must utilize this. In comparing the top two female throwers of the late 1990s, German biomechanist Dr. Klaus Bartonietz found that former World record holder Mihaela Melinte was able to produce better results than her rival Olga Kuzenkova, even though Kuzenkova had a longer double-support phase.[23] The reason was that despite the shorter acceleration path used by Melinte, she displayed much more power during the throw, which allowed as much or more acceleration in a shorter time span. Later in her career, Kuzenkova increased her results, even while her double-support phase became shorter. Bartonietz attributes this to an increase of power that was greater than the loss of technique. Simply increasing double support, and the amount of time available to transfer energy to the hammer, is only half of the equation. As important as the length of double support is how much energy an athlete transfers during it.

The discussion of power is also relevant to whether an athlete uses three or four turns. A fourth turn gives a thrower additional time to accelerate the hammer. A three-turn throw, on the other hand, requires immense energy to be transferred to the throw during each double-support phase. This, in turn, requires immense power since power is the rate at which energy is added to the hammer. An extra turn, if used appropriately, requires less power each turn to produce the same result. In addition to an athlete's physiological profile, this is an important consideration when deciding to use three or four turns.

Newer studies have looked at the transfer of energy from a new angle and tried to trace the kinetic chain to see how energy moves sequentially through the body to the hammer. After observing several elite female throwers including world record holder Betty Heidler, then University of Konstanz doctoral candidate Marwa Sakr found that the kinetic energy of the hammer consistently increased from the high point through the end of the double-support phase in all athletes.[23]

Also, as expected, the body's kinetic energy increases earlier than the hammer's since the energy is generated by the body before being transferred to the hammer. However, the amount of delay between the two was the interesting part. The body's kinetic energy increased much earlier, beginning at the low point of the previous turn and continuing to increase all the way to the high point. After the high point, the body's kinetic energy then begins to decrease. In other words, it appears the body is creating energy already during single support and then it is being transferred to the hammer during double support.

THE BALL & CHAIN

• • •

Torque. Whenever there is talk about generating power in any throwing event, torque inevitably comes up. Discus technique in particular aims to get an athlete in a position where the body leads the implement throughout the throw before the arm and implement are whipped around at the release in order to generate speed. Use of similar toque technique was a mainstay of hammer technique until the Soviets brought forward the new model.

Under the Soviet model, hammer throwers still have torque between the hip axis and shoulder axis, but not at the extreme that once existed. The body in large part works together with only small deviations between the orientation of the hips, shoulders, head, and hammer. During Yuriy Sedykh's throw, his hips were consistently in front of the shoulder axis until the release, but the variation between the maximum and minimum amount of torque during each throw ranged only 30º. For example, he might have begun double-support with a 45º differential and ended double-support with just a 15º differential.[24]

Torque is good since it can help acceleration, but there is only so much the body can do with it. If there is too much torque, then the negative consequences, such as leading or dragging the hammer, start to outweigh the benefits. The goal is for the hammer to lead or drag as little as possible, since both positions reduce the radius of the hammer. As demonstrated by Sedykh, a minimal amount of torque seems ideal since it can still be used to generate power without bringing the negative side effects with it.

• • •

Competing Forces. There are many competing forces in the throw. For example, pulling up on the hammer as it rises or down on the hammer as it descends will create angular forces that can accelerate the hammer. However, at the same time, such a movement can decrease the radius and path of force application available to the thrower.

The hammer is also moving in three dimensions, which creates other competing forces. Therefore, in addition to measuring horizontal force, you also need to measure vertical force. Olympic and World Champion Koji Murofushi, who has also earned a doctorate, teamed up with his colleagues to show that both the hammer and the body are moving in two asynchronous rhythms throughout the throw.[25] As he notes, the principle that accelerates the hammer is similar to the way that a pendulum increases in speed when it is pulled upward against the downward movement of the swinging weight. While moving in opposite directions, they work in harmony to accelerate the implement.

• • •

Murofushi's idea is one of the best at bringing science together with practice. In addition to a bunch of numbers, his study and many of the others listed above also aim to help coaches and athletes understand what is happening during the throw. Just like video analysis can focus too much on positions, biomechanical analysis can focus too much on numbers and graphs. Murofushi puts it in context like every coach should: throwing the hammer is also about movements, but numbers can help with that too.

PART IV //

TRAINING

11 // EXERCISE SELECTION

Constructing a training plan consists of two main steps: first selecting exercises to perform, and then arranging them in a way to provide the most benefit to each training session, training period, and season. I will only briefly discuss the second step, better known as periodization, in this final section. The focus of this section will instead be on understanding some of the general concepts of training for the hammer throw and how they influence exercise selection. Exercises are, after all, the first step in constructing a plan. They are the tools of training that help a thrower progress. And without the right tools, it is impossible to build anything, no matter how good the design.

• • •

Bondarchuk popularized an exercise classification system for all sports that has proven so useful that large national federations such as UK Athletics have adopted it in their education materials. Bondarchuk classifies exercises along a spectrum of specificity. Under this system, all exercises fall into one of four categories:

General Preparatory Exercises. These exercises use both energy systems and movements different from the athlete's competitive event. For a hammer thrower, an example of this would be long-distance jogging. Jogging is a primarily aerobic exercise using linear movement. The hammer throw, on the other hand, is a rotational movement utilizing mostly the alactic anaerobic energy system.

Specific Preparatory Exercises. This category of exercises is closer to the competitive event in that they use the same muscles and systems, but in the form of a different movement. An example of this for the hammer throw would be the back squat. The legs are utilized in both the back squat and the hammer throw. The difference is the movement pattern.

Specific Developmental Exercises. This group, often referred to as "specific strength" or "special strength," combines the same muscles and systems as the competitive event, as well as parts of the competition movements. An example for the hammer throw could be winding and releasing a heavy hammer or executing twisting movements while holding a plate. Both exercises use the same muscles and systems as the hammer throw and mimic different parts of the whole movement: the releases mimic the release movement and the plate twists mimic the twisting movement in the throw. Exercises in this group also often tend to be heavier than the competition exercise in order to strengthen the muscles used in the movements.

Competitive Exercise. The name of this category is self-explanatory. This group includes the competitive event and slight variations. For a hammer throw, this category would include throwing the competition-weight hammer with the full technique, as well as under- or over-weight hammers with full technique.

• • •

There are a few things to point out when looking at Bondarchuk's exercise classification system. First, the classification of an exercise is entirely dependent on what event the athlete is training for. What might be considered a specific development exercise for a hammer thrower could be a specific preparatory exercise for the javelin throw or even a general preparatory exercise for a marathon runner.

Second, the groups of exercises become progressively more event-specific as they move from the general preparatory exercises to competitive exercises. As this happens, the number of exercises to choose from in each category decreases. While there are nearly unlimited exercises that are general in nature, the hammer throw is such an exact movement that there are only a few so close in nature that they would be classified as a competitive exercise or specific developmental exercise.

Third, as training exercises become more specific, they also allow for the simultaneous development of both the technique and physical elements of the event. Specific and general preparatory exercises, on the other hand, prepare the body to meet the demands of training and contain no technical element.

• • •

The value of classifying exercises by specificity becomes apparent when you look at another one of Bondarchuk's concepts: the transfer of training. Transfer of training analyzes how an improvement in results in one exercise impacts results in another exercise or event. If improvement in one exercise causes improvement in another exercise, that exercise is said to have a positive transfer. If the results in another exercise are unaffected or decline, then the first exercise has a neutral or negative transfer with respect to the second exercise.

The transfer of training works better in theory than in practice because it can be quite difficult to identify the exact cause-and-effect chain associated with improved performance. Within a training plan, an athlete executes dozens of exercises each day. With so many variables, attempting to determine which exercise or exercises among the group actually causes an increase in results in the competition exercise is difficult.

THE BALL & CHAIN

All coaches utilize "transfer of training," whether they are familiar with the term or not. When constructing a training program, a coach must decide which exercises to use and which exercises to leave out. That decision always comes down to what the coach thinks will help the athlete throw farther or run faster or jump higher. Because finding the cause-and-effect relationship is difficult, some coaches base their decisions on intuition, experience, or on science.

Science normally proves no better than intuition or experience at finding direct causation, but it can help in measuring the correlation between exercises. The correlation is the way in which results of different exercises rise and fall together, and while correlation comes with its own set of problems, it can still be a good solution to the problem.

The trouble with correlations is that they are often misleading. For example, imagine an athlete that includes bicep curls in a training program and thereafter throws a personal best. We all know there is no reason the bicep curls should cause a personal best in the hammer throw, but nevertheless the correlation between curls and hammer throwing would be high for this athlete.

In fact, all exercises the athlete improves during the same time would have a high correlation and it is likely that one or more of these other exercises is, in fact, helping the athlete throw farther. This problem can be mitigated somewhat by more data. By looking at lots of athletes or lots of training data from the same athlete, you begin to see that bicep strength has no real positive effect. This is because while the two may have risen together in one instance, it is not always the case. The more cases you look at, the more likely you will find which exercises frequently improve together. The exercises that maintain a high correlation over a large sample size are the exercises that most likely actually caused the improved results.

Bondarchuk did just this to analyze the transfer of training among hammer throwers. After coaching, overseeing, and testing thousands of hammer throwers over more than four decades of coaching, his studies concluded that a positive transfer is most often observed where an exercise is similar in form and content to the competitive exercise. This means that exercises in both the specific developmental exercises and competitive exercises categories tend to have a higher transfer and help increase results the most. The next two chapters explore these categories further.

12 // SPECIFIC DEVELOPMENTAL EXERCISES

From the athletic world to the corporate world you will hear people preaching the mantra "stronger is better." This statement pretty much holds up, but unfortunately the people saying it don't always understand what it means. Stronger is better, as long as it is the right type of strength.

Most people making this statement in the athletic world are referring to general strength as the type of strength that will make you better. In some sense this is true in the hammer throw: general overall strength is a necessary component of success since you need to be strong to throw the hammer far. In addition, gains in general strength for beginners can quickly lead to longer throws. However, relying on this theory too much can be troublesome as general strength alone is not enough to throw far.

After a certain base level of strength is attained, general strength has a point of diminishing returns where its correlation to success drops off. Just as in the financial world, training has both short-term and long-term investments. Focusing on traditional general strength training is a great short-term investment. As mentioned above, a young athlete that adds

THE BALL & CHAIN

TABLE 3: CORRELATIONS WITH THE HAMMER

Competition Result	Clean	Snatch	Squat	Vertical Jump	Long Jump
60-65m Men	0.421	0.451	0.437	0.360	0.397
75-80m Men	0.270	0.245	0.196	0.124	0.127
55-60m Women	0.542	0.590	0.524	0.368	0.256
70-75m Women	0.512	0.460	0.340	0.324	0.326

strength can quickly improve results. However, over the long-term, the results plateau with this approach.

Once again the research of Bondarchuk is a good guide in this area. His studies compared two groups of athletes: one group focused on lifting heavy and the other focused more on throwing-specific exercises. While the first group made faster progress in the beginning, the second group inevitably surpassed the first group after about four years.[26] General strength was just not enough to throw far.

To illustrate this in detail, consider the numbers compiled in Bondarchuk's research. Table 3 above shows that for a 60- to 65-meter male hammer thrower, the squat has a correlation of 0.437 to competitive results. With 0.00 as a neutral correlation and 1.00 as a perfect correlation, this is a very significant number.[27] In fact, it's correlation is nearly as high as throwing the heavy 10-kilogram hammer as shown later in Table 4. However, you immediately see a stark difference when comparing these correlations with that of a world class 75- to 80-meter thrower. There, the squat has a correlation of just 0.196 and is no longer statistically significant. While the correlations are slightly higher for women, you can see the same trend.

Rather than disproving the "stronger is better" theory, this clarification just brings us back to my original point: stronger is better, as long as it is the right type of strength. The right type of strength for the hammer throw is hammer-specific strength, not just general strength. Hammer-specific strength, such as the ability to throw the 10-kilogram hammer, is needed. Table 4 illustrates that the need for this type of strength becomes even more important as an athlete improves. The need for general strength such as heavy squatting, on the other hand, generally decreases. Building hammer-specific strength requires different exercises and relies heavily on specific developmental exercises since they fill the gap between specific preparatory exercises such as the squat and actually throwing the hammer.

• • •

World-record holder Yuriy Sedykh is the classic example of someone who benefited from this type of strength. The first impression he left on spectators was never an imposing one, even at the height of his career. Most people viewed him as rather lean since his American and German competitors would often outweigh him by 20 kilograms or more. He was also less than intimidating in the weight room, where his lifts paled in comparison to the astronomical amounts being hoisted by others in the 1980s. As a result, few people considered Sedykh "strong" within the normal sense of the word.

Throwing a hammer over 86 meters requires a thrower to exert over 700 pounds (317.5 kilograms) of centripetal force on the hammer ball.[28] You have to be strong to do this. Watching Sedykh handle the hammer with such ease in the ring left no doubt about his strength levels, no matter how much he could squat or snatch.

When you change the definition of strength, you see that Sedykh was not only as strong as his competitors, but stronger in the exercises that mattered more. For example, he had a personal best of 70.20 meters with the heavy 10-kilogram hammer and regularly did plate twists in training while holding two or more 25-kilogram plates extended in front of his body. Hammer-specific strength, rather than a great clean and jerk, is one reason why he was able to accelerate the ball better with three turns than anyone else could with four turns. That's the reason why he holds the world record and dominated his competition.

•••

While there are fewer specific development exercises than specific preparatory exercises, there are still more than enough for a coach to choose from. The definition of this class of exercises is still quite inclusive: an exercise must simply use the same muscles, systems, and one or more of the movements of the hammer throw. With such a broad definition, there are still hundreds of exercises a hammer thrower can utilize.

Over the years I have done exercises with hammers, weights, medicine balls, kettlebells, and other equipment. I have even used such unconventional tools as car tires, rocks, sandbags, and a variety of other pieces of homemade equipment. The coach's biggest limitation is imagination. Yet despite this, some of my favorite exercises are also among the simplest.

Twists. There are so many variations of this exercise that it never gets old, since it best mimics the motion of the throw and the acceleration happening in the double-support phase. The traditional hammer thrower's plate twist is done while holding a plate in front of the body with the arms extended parallel to the ground. Then simply twist from side to side. But this exercise can also be done while holding a dumbbell, with a bar on the back, or in a variety of other ways. The simple twisting motion remains the same with a slight change in the execution.

Releases. Specific developmental exercises do not need to be confined to the weight room. Throwers can use a medicine ball, kettlebell, dumbbell, or even a heavy rock to mimic the release and focus on developing strength in that part of the throw. One of the advantage to exercises with a release is that all of the energy can be focused on accelerating the implement and generating power. In exercises without a release, such as the twist, energy is expended both accelerating and decelerating the implement with each repetition.

FIGURE 9: SPECIAL DEVELOPMENTAL EXERCISE - PLATE TWIST

Hammer Drills. Exercises also do not need to be limited to special equipment. Simply picking up the hammer can also be a good way to isolate a part of the throw and is an easy method of developing hammer-specific strength. Winding or turning with heavy hammers or a similar homemade device can be helpful, as are releases with heavy hammers or weights.

As I mentioned above, this is only the starting point. Numerous other exercises exist and even these exercises can be varied by adding additional orbit, doing them while seated, with one hand, with both hands, with a different implement, or any number of other variations. The key is to use exercises that use the same muscles as the throw and contain parts of the full throwing movement of the throws. Attention to detail is important here.

THE BALL & CHAIN

FIGURE 10: SPECIAL DEVELOPMENTAL EXERCISE - HEAVY WINDS

• • •

Implementing specific developmental exercises into training is quite easy. The simplest method is to just spend five minutes on an exercise at the end of each throwing session. But a more thoughtful approach helps even more. Here are a few guidelines I use for incorporating special development exercises into training:

Timing. It is best to focus on specific developmental exercises after the throwing session. Exercises performed before throwing might tire the athlete and make it more difficult to focus on and improve hammer technique.

Simplicity. Utilizing too many specific developmental exercises at once can be overkill. Choosing one or two good exercises and periodically rotating them is the best solution. I will discuss variation in more detail in Chapter 14, but for now it is enough to say that simplicity helps.

Weight. The weight you choose can be fairly arbitrary. You want to have enough weight so that the athlete can feel the implement and increase strength, but you also do not want so much weight that the athlete's technique suffers, leading to an injury or bad habits. In addition, too much weight can also fatigue the athlete and negatively affect technique in subsequent throwing sessions. Other than with youth athletes, I would not recommend using weights lighter than 9 kilograms (20 pounds) for mature boys or 5 kilograms (11 pounds) for mature girls in kettlebell, medicine ball, or weight throw exercises. Beyond that, you just need to see how the athlete reacts to different implements and find the right fit. What is important is that they are using specific developmental exercises consistently. The weight is less significant.

Volume. Again, consistency trumps not just the weight used, but the volume of specific developmental exercises in each training session. Both the effect of the weight and daily volume are compounded when repeated on a consistent basis. As little as two to three sets of 10 repetitions each session with a specific developmental exercises will lead to solid long-term specific strength gains.

Even when my training reaches its highest volume of specific strength work, the volume in each individual session remains less than overwhelming. For example, in one training program, I performed six sets of 10 repetitions with 25-kilogram plate twists at each session. This volume was something I could easily complete, but after a 10-session training week I suddenly had amassed a total of 16.5 tons of volume each week from plate twists alone. This program was at the extreme for me, which means that even low or moderate volume will still produce substantial loads when performed consistently over time.

Intensity. Throwing the hammer at high intensities is important since a crucial element of technical training is to ensure technique holds up at those speeds. This is less important with special developmental exercises. While higher intensities will produce more power, there are also some downsides. There is only so much high intensity work that athletes can do, and it is better to concentrate on more important elements like throwing. Reducing the intensity to medium or low levels still allows the development of strength and also helps develop other qualities like range of motion, stress reflexology, posture, and patience; it can also assist in recovery.

• • •

This chapter gave some ideas on how to incorporate specific developmental exercises into your training in order to improve specific strength. However, perhaps the best way to develop special strength is even easier: throw the hammer. Often viewed simply as technical training, throwing is the most dynamic and versatile strength exercise available to hammer throwers and should not be overlooked.

13 // THROWING AS TRAINING

Throwing is a more widely utilized training exercise for the hammer throw when compared to specific developmental exercises. After all, we wouldn't be hammer throwers if we didn't actually throw something. Many elite throwers will take a minimum of 5,000 throws a year and commonly more than 10,000 with various different implements. If a thrower only has time to do one exercise in training, throwing is the clear choice.

Many coaches view throwing simply as a chance to develop technique. Throwing is actually the most versatile training exercise available since it improves many aspects of the throw at once. Runners don't think of running as a way to just develop technique. To them, it is also a way for them to build endurance, strength, and other qualities needed to succeed. And, while cross-training with a bicycle might develop their leg muscles and improve their cardiovascular and respiratory systems, few runners would argue that the majority of training time should be spent on a bike; though similar in some ways, cycling does not transfer as well to running.

Conversely, too many coaches think of throwing as a way to just improve technique and look elsewhere for ways to increase the other elements of a good throw. This leads to training programs where the vast majority

THE BALL & CHAIN

of time is spent outside of the ring. Throwing itself is the best specific strength exercise available and this should be kept in mind when designing a training plan.

In addition, while exercises in all other categories focus primarily on building strength or fitness or flexibility or another single element, those in the competitive exercise category simultaneously train all the qualities needed in the throw. Most importantly, this allows power and technique to develop alongside one another, which has proven an effective way to increase power and distance in the throw. For high-level athletes in particular, it is difficult to transfer gains from exercises that work on one element into the complete movement. Developing the qualities together eliminates this problem.

Combined, these factors make throwing itself one of the most versatile training tools available to a coach. There is no excuse not to make different variations of throwing the primary exercises in any training program.

• • •

I mention variations since the competitive exercises category also includes slight variations of the competitive movement. This opens the door for throwing various other implements with the same technique, namely hammers that are lighter or heavier. There are advantages to both.

Like specific developmental exercises, light and heavy hammers offer a very high correlation to results with the competition hammer. In fact, the correlation is almost always significantly higher than any weight room exercise. Throwing the competition-weight hammer in training should ideally have a perfect correlation to competition results just as doing push ups in training should correlate to how well you could do them in a competition.

Light and heavy hammers also have very strong correlations, often two or three times higher than traditional weight room exercises like the squat or clean, but despite this, their use in training is more controversial. Many top throwers stray only rarely from the competition weight hammer in training. Many either see no reason to move too far from the competition hammer, or are worried that a change might affect the finely-tuned rhythm they have developed with the competition hammer. While the rhythm may be affected and other adverse effects could arise, the benefits far outweigh the downsides, especially if the thrower and coach are alert and watchful. Having other hammers means having more exercises to choose from and a better chance for variety to help the body to continue to adapt and improve.

• • •

Light hammers are generally accepted as good training tool by coaches around the world. If you want to throw farther, you need to be able to maintain the same technique while moving faster. Throwing light hammers accomplishes this. At the same time, even though a hammer is light it still helps develop specific strength. While it might not develop as much strength as a competition weight or heavy hammer, it will still develop the throwing muscles on each throw and the lighter weight can even allow an increased volume of throws to improve technique and strength for a longer amount of time at each training session.

As shown in Tables 4 and 5, the correlations for light hammer tend to be higher for beginning and intermediate throwers, making it a perfect tool to use as throwers move up the ranks.[29] Also note that the correlations with all alternative hammers are significantly higher than the correlations of weight room exercises discussed in the last chapter.

• • •

Heavy hammers, on the other hand, have a higher correlation among elite throwers. Unlike light hammers, the use of heavier hammers is not universally accepted by throwers and coaches. And the heavier the hammer is, the more controversial the topic becomes. The fear is that as the weight increases, technique must be compromised, thereby creating bad habits. If

TABLE 4: CORRELATIONS BETWEEN DIFFERENT HAMMER WEIGHTS FOR MEN

Level of Thrower	5kg	6kg	8kg	9kg	10kg
60 to 65 meters	0.824	0.786	0.869	0.675	0.542
75 to 80 meters	0.564	0.664	0.798	0.765	0.824

TABLE 5: CORRELATIONS BETWEEN DIFFERENT HAMMER WEIGHTS FOR WOMEN

Level of Thrower	3kg	5kg	6kg
50 to 60 meters	0.724	0.825	0.876
70 to 75 meters	0.650	0.920	0.950

not properly monitored, this can indeed occur. Therefore, coaches need to ensure that athletes focus on technique as much with heavy implements as they do with other implements. If technique falters too much, then the implement is too heavy and its use becomes counterproductive. For each athlete the limit is different and can change over time as strength and technique evolve.

Personally, I do not find this a difficult task in my throws. Heavier hammers make for slower throws, and a slower throw gives me more time to focus and react throughout the throw. I often find my technical flaws are amplified not by heavy hammers, but by light hammers since I focus on the speed of the body rather than patience and technique. I've also noticed this with the younger athletes I coach as long as their base level of strength is enough to handle the increased forces of the heavier hammers.

As Tables 4 and 5 show, heavy hammers have the highest correlation for elite athletes. The 10-kilogram hammer offers male throwers over 75 meters a higher correlation than any other implement. The same can be said for women over 65 meters and the 6-kilogram hammer. Don't be afraid to use heavy hammers.

•••

As an alternative to heavy hammers, many coaches use short heavy hammers. By shortening the hammer wire, the speed of the throw increases making it once again feel more like a light hammer. While this adds a new element to training, this might be one area where additional choices overcomplicate things.

Shorter hammers minimize the strength benefit of the heavy hammer. But more importantly, they also drastically changes the hammer's orbit. World-class thrower Sergey Litvinov Jr. put it best when he said,

> The difference between the standard length 5-kilogram hammer and standard length 7.26-kilogram hammer is the rhythm and speed. The orbit and the technique stay the same; everything is just faster with a 5-kilogram hammer. But with hammers of two different lengths the difference is that the technique is very different. One has a push action and the other pulling. The body saves this feeling. A short hammer can be used as an exercise, but it is not like a similar throws session.[30]

Again, if the technique does not falter, there is no real reason to shorten the implement. The orbit is one of the most important aspects of training and throwing normal-length heavy hammers with good technique will provide the benefits you are looking for without as many negative consequences.

•••

In addition to all of the benefits listed earlier in this chapter, perhaps the biggest advantage of throwing light or heavy hammers is that they simply provide variety. The body needs to be continually challenged with new stresses in order to adapt, improve, and ultimately throw farther. Heavy and light hammers provide the opportunity to change training enough

THE BALL & CHAIN

to stimulate the adaptation process without shifting the focus of training so much as to destroy the balance of training and prevent technical improvement. This topic of change is quite important and must be used wisely in training. The next chapter discusses how change, along with four other concepts, explain the difference between training and training with a plan.

14 // ADVANCED TRAINING CONCEPTS

In the preceding chapters, I've discussed many aspects for training, from technique to strength and speed. To acquire these aspects, many more elements are required like proper coaching, a grasp of sports sciences, and exercise selection. Exercises can then be broken down into categories like throwing the hammer, throwing other implements, weight room exercises, jumping, sprinting, and numerous other categories. As important as each of these aspects are, there is one aspect of a successful throw that might trump everything: confidence.

Nothing is more energizing than knowing you are fit, strong, and can throw far on any given day. Confidence facilitates relaxation and this will get a thrower into a better zone quicker and more consistently than any sports psychologist can. When you pick up a hammer with confidence, you completely control it; you can do anything you want to with it.

Confidence for a hammer throw comes from creating a plan that combines all other aspects of training in the best way possible. A strong plan will produce results and that in turn produces confidence in an athlete's training. Confidence in training then quickly turns into confidence at competitions.

THE BALL & CHAIN

· · ·

As the cliché goes, creating a good plan is easier said than done. In an ideal world, we could create a plan that produces continuous improvement. But in reality, no matter how good the plan is, every athlete inevitably has bad days and even bad months. The key to keeping confidence throughout the bad days is to create a plan that anticipates the ups and downs and uses them to make even greater gains. Bad days are necessary, and when they are anticipated, confidence will not falter. In fact, an athlete often gains confidence from knowing the plan is working and that they know exactly when they will be throwing far.

Putting together a plan for the hammer thrower sounds like a complex endeavor since it must combine all the aspects of training listed above. It must combine a focus on improving technique with a focus on improving strength. And, to top it all off, everything must be combined in a way that will ensure the athlete can produce the best results on a few pre-planned days. I spent years searching for the secret of putting all the components together and found out that my search was futile. There is no secret; it's just common sense. If you look at the training of the top athletes in nearly every sport, their methods differ but their training almost always focuses on many of the same basic principles.

This chapter will provide an overview of five training concepts that are an essential first step towards creating a long-term training plan in the hammer throw. While continuous improvement may not be possible in any circumstance, coaches and athletes can still aim for the Japanese ideal of *kaizen*. *Kaizen* is the practice of focusing on the continuous improvement of processes and methods. The method can keep improving in all circumstances since the concepts below must be continuously reapplied.

· · ·

Concept 1: Individuality. One thing I have not provided in this book is the perfect training program for hammer throw. The reason is that it does not exist. There is no one perfect training plan. Just as technique has to be adapted to the strengths and weaknesses and individual peculiarities of each athlete, so does training. When given a specific set of exercises, each athlete responds differently. Some will take longer to adapt, some will adapt quicker. Some will see greater gains, while others might even regress. The only thing in common is that they are different.

A recent study of swimmers helps explain how big of a role individuality should play. Researchers at the University of Alabama took a small sample of elite swimmers and gave them three different warm up variations to try: a normal long warm up, a short warm up, and no warm up.[31] After each warm up they performed a time trial. Unsurprisingly, the normal warm up generally proved the best option among the three warm ups. However, the normal warm up was only the best for 44 percent (44%) of the athletes. Another 19 percent (19%) performed better with a short warm up and 37 percent (37%) performed the best without a warm-up. What was best for the group in general was actually worse for the majority of athletes. As the authors pointed out, "[i]t is important to note that the swimmers compete individually and not as a group mean."

The same logic is applicable to the various correlations mentioned in the previous two chapters. These are correlations for a group of hammer throwers. Each individual may have higher or lower correlations than this group. While you can learn what is best for a group in a book, no book will tell you what is best for a specific athlete. To do that, the coach must observe his athletes, learn from them, keep detailed records, and adjust training accordingly. This can take a year or more, but it is worth it in the long run because the coach will have a better understanding of the athlete's individual physiology.

An example of interpreting individuality into training comes once again from Bondarchuk. Bondarchuk began to coach the 2011 World Championship shot put silver medalist Dylan Armstrong back in 2005, as Armstrong was switching events from the hammer throw to the shot put. At that point in his career Armstrong had already achieved an amazing level of general strength, but he also had little special strength and technique to go with it. The reason was that he had taken relatively few throws with the shot put before 2005. To address this, Armstrong's training focused seventy percent (70%) on technique and thirty percent (30%) on specific strength. Almost no time was spent on general strength. Every element of training, including the exercises and the time spent on each area, were also tailored specifically to Armstrong. After six years, Armstrong was ranked first in the world in his new event.

With beginners or weaker athletes, on the other hand, I doubt Bondarchuk would have put together the same training plan. Instead these athletes might need more focus on general strength. But the formula isn't just as easy as targeting an athlete's weaknesses. Many times it does help to eliminate weaknesses. This was the case with Armstrong; there was no need for him to strengthen a strength when doing so would give him no advantage. Adding another 10 pounds to his massive bench press would not have helped him throw farther. But adding technique or special strength helped him tremendously.

For other athletes, it might make sense to focus even more on a strength to maximize its benefit. Justin Rodhe came to Bondarchuk as a shot putter with another skill set: great special strength but relatively poor general strength. Rather than attacking his general strength weakness, Bondarchuk and Rodhe simply leveraged his great special strength to produce yet another 21-meter shot putter. In other cases, it makes no sense to turn a precision thrower into a power thrower when they just don't have the engine. For these athletes, tailoring training to both utilize and amplify their strengths can be the best solution.

In rare cases, strengths and weaknesses can work together. Athletes can sometimes emphasize a strength to eliminate a weakness. In other words, you can kill two birds with one stone. Before he became the world record holder, Ashton Eaton's biggest weakness was the throwing events. While he didn't need to become an amazing thrower, coach Harry Marra knew he needed to become good enough that those events were not a liability in competitions. In the shot put, he had never looked comfortable using the standard glide technique. Marra, one day, decided to switch things up after noticing something in practice. In the long jump, high jump, and pole vault, Eaton always jumped off the left leg, but in the shot put he was required to initiate the movement with his right leg. Marra then switched to an unconventional start to utilize the strength in Eaton's left leg. It worked and got rid of his biggest liability. His throwing events were still his weakest events, but he nevertheless set a world record.

These examples are varied, but show that each athlete has a different formula for success. Creating a program individualized to a specific athlete takes time to set up, but it also allows for optimal training.

• • •

Concept 2: Understand the need for both change and regularity. Without adaptation, the body would never improve. On its own the body loves homeostasis and has many processes in place to ensure a stable internal environment. Athletes, on the other hand, want progress. They want to improve technique, improve strength, and gain muscle. To do this, the body needs to change.

Back in 1936, Austrian-Canadian scientist Hans Selye first outlined his influential theory on general adaptation syndrome.[32] His theory stated that when confronted by a new stress that disrupts homeostasis the body first reacts in an alarm stage where the body's resources are mobilized to meet the stress. Next, the body response stabilizes the system reaching a new level of homeostasis. If the stress continues, the body may reach a third level of exhaustion where the body can no longer resist the stress.

While Selye's work referred to all types of stress applied to an organism, the same principles apply in training since training is just the process of intentionally placing planned amounts of stress on an athlete's body. If you present the body with a new exercise, it will at first be difficult until the body mobilizes its resources, changes itself, and tries to improve so that the exercise no longer feels as difficult. If all goes as planned, the body has reached a new, higher level where the stress is no longer stressful. This process is called adaptation, and in order to continue improvement, you need constant stress. In other words, you need continuous change. Research has continued on adaptation and moved beyond this model, but Seyle's theories were revolutionary in that they explained a scientific basis for how training worked and coaches soon designed training methods to harness adaptation.

Russian scientist L.P. Mateyev was one of the first people to apply Seyle's work to physical preparation methods. Most importantly, Mateyev discovered the cyclical nature of form development. [3] Bondarchuk then continued this research and demonstrated that athletes using standard training methods would experience a plateau in performances after 4 to 6 years of training. This was due to a lack of change in training exercises. While the weights were being changed, the exercises remained the same and left the body with fewer new stresses to adapt to. Accordingly, when an athlete reaches the peak in his respective developmental model, training exercises must be changed in order to continue improvement and prevent a performance plateau.

To illustrate this concept, take a simple example of using a program of 50 push ups a day to become better at doing push ups. If you used this program you would quickly notice that, after an initial improvement, the body will reach a plateau as it adapts to doing push ups. In order to continue to progress, the body will need a new stimulus, e.g. a new exercise to adapt to. If, after a month, you start doing the bench press, the change will allow your body to overcome that plateau, by doing a different exercise that still works towards the goal. When you return to doing push ups, your body will be at a higher level and be able to adapt, once again, to push ups since the exercise is no longer stale.

Combining multiple exercises together at once will also be helpful. More exercises mean more stress, and the body is required to adapt even more. However, more exercises will also extend the amount of time required for adaptation since the body has more to adapt to. The change can be subtle (switching from an 8-kilogram to a 9-kilogram hammer in training), but some type of change is ultimately necessary to prevent stagnation.

The timing of the change is also important. One must balance the need for change in a training program against the need for regularity. If, rather than doing a constant routine of 50 push ups each day, you try a new exercise every day, the body will no longer have time to adapt to the old exercises before it is forced to adapt to the new ones. Rather than improving, results could stall or even regress. The more constant the stress, the better the body can react and adapt to it.

The best programs are those that are able to negotiate the body's needs for both change and regularity, a formula which is different for each athlete.

• • •

Concept 3: Prioritization. When writing a training plan, coaches have four categories of exercises to choose from, as described in Chapter 11. Combined, these categories have a near infinite number of exercises. Athletes, on the other hand, have a finite amount of time and energy. Therefore, just as coaches must prioritize technical changes, they must prioritize elements of training. In this sense, it may be helpful for a coach to think about choosing exercises like they would an investment decision. The best investors cannot invest in everything since they have a set amount of money. Instead they must choose the best options and diversify among them. Rather than money, the coach is investing other finite items: the athlete's time and energy. Coaches should look for the best exercises, i.e. those that produce the best return on investment for the time and energy available.

There is a double effect of choosing a bad investment. Not only do you end up with less than what you started with if the investment decreases in value, but you have way less than you would have had with a better investment. This is known as an "opportunity cost" in economics. To illustrate its relation to training, take the example of the bench press. While the bench press may not directly hurt results for a hammer thrower, the time and energy put into it will tire an athlete and will take the place of an exercise that might help substantially. In some cases, no exercise might even be better since it can allow the body to rest and recover more. Selecting an exercise should not be done in a vacuum; it should always be done with an eye on the alternatives so that the opportunity cost is taken into account.

The previous three chapters have clearly outlined what I feel are the best investments. Investing in general strength may provide good short-term gains, but over the long term special developmental exercises and throwing the hammer provide the most benefit. Runners run in training. Sprinters sprint. Jumpers jump. And throwers should throw. Nothing else develops the muscles and movements of the throw like throwing itself. The weight room should not be the home base of training for a hammer thrower.

But, the weight room does play a role. Elite throwers still need a base level of strength to throw far. While this is fairly easy to attain, it still requires general weight training, and hammer throwers should regularly do variations of the snatch and clean, squats, and other traditional lifts. The volume and intensity should not distract from the primary exercises, but should still be enough to make gains. A high-volume squat workout, for example, will tire your legs and make attempts to improve technique unproductive. A quick low or medium-intensity workout, on the other hand, has the right balance of priorities to add strength while still allowing the body to recover and continue to focus on many more important exercises like throwing.

• • •

Concept 4: Be analytical. Science is our friend. Coaches do not need to be scientists, but they at least need to embrace the methods of scientific analysis. This starts with proper data collection. Trial and error can be a great way to create a training plan, but without data it will not be as effective. Coaches cannot truly confirm whether their methods are working unless they have data to back it up. Therefore, it is imperative that coaches maintain detailed daily records of every exercise the athlete performs, the volume and intensity of each workout, and the athlete's best daily throwing performances. Elements outside of training can also be recorded, such as how well an athlete is sleeping and their energy or motivation levels. By looking back at these notes, you can begin to see what worked and what didn't no matter what type of training plan you are using.

As in science, the quest for the perfect throw and perfect training plan in the hammer throw is never-ending. The minute a coach thinks they understand everything about an athlete or about a concept is the same minute they stop improving as a coach. My two biggest mentors, Bondarchuk and Connolly, studied the event as much at age 70 as they did when they began their coaching or throwing careers. This, combined with their willingness to try new things, led them to continue to evolve their ideas over several decades and produce successful training systems. They always knew there were more answers out there waiting to be found.

•••

Concept 5: Technique comes first. I save this point for last so that it might leave a lasting impression to be emphasized at each training session: while a good training program is important, it means little without good technique. World record holder Yuriy Sedykh had great specific strength, but more importantly he also had what most biomechanics agree is the most efficient technique in the history of the hammer throw. All the different types of strength mean nothing unless the athlete is able to transfer the energy to the hammer. Technique is the means by which the athlete does that. An athlete or coach should never overlook the big picture.

•••

Successfully combining these elements is where science meets art. Blending these principles into a unique mixture allows a coach to add his or her own creativity to the sport and also helps an athlete perform the best. It is what makes the hammer throw one of the most interesting and exciting sports in the world.

And while throwers have won gold medals and set Olympic records using a variety of methods, they all have these principles in common. Perhaps, a new method will provide a better path to 90 meters for men and 80 meters for women. Chances are that this method will still combine the same key principles of training. Understand them, and you will be off to a great start as a coach.

EPILOGUE

This book started with a discussion of my philosophy of hammer throwing: speed. It is only right that I come back to it in the end. All of the chapters in between have dissected various elements of this amazing sport, from learning to throw all the way to the complexities of biomechanics and training methodology. But while each chapter looked deeper and deeper into the event, the focus remained primarily on speed.

Speed is the common point connecting the process of learning technique, studying the science of the event, and deciding what exercise to use in training. What do you need to do differently in the technique to help the ball go faster? How can physics help you along the way? What exercises will help you push the ball better and faster? These are all crucial questions.

Coaches should be skeptics. When questioned about any aspect of training, they should be able to give a response about how it connects to this philosophy or their own philosophy. And they need to reanalyze the questions constantly to make sure they are finding the best solution possible. If they find themselves speechless, then they need to examine if that element really belongs in training.

• • •

This process of skepticism is an ongoing endeavor. While the best throws are often described by throwers as "effortless," the effort never ends. Effort is always needed as hammer throwers are perfectionists. We are always trying to focus on something that will make the next throw better than the last. I do not know any elite throwers that walk into the ring and try to focus on absolutely nothing since improvement never happens by going through the motions. Even if the athlete is thinking about relaxing, they are still thinking about something and asking themselves how they can get better at it. This process gets harder as athletes get better. Philosopher Barbara Gail Montero makes the point even better when writing in the *New York Times* about her experience as a dancer:

> Ballet, I knew, never gets easier; if anything, it gets harder, because as you develop as a dancer you develop both stricter standards for what counts as good dancing and your ability to evaluate your dancing, finding flaws that previously went unnoticed. . . . The ability to see room for improvement, however, is not of much use unless one also has a strong and continuing desire to improve. . . . And improving, especially after you have acquired a high level of skill, typically requires an enormous amount of effort. Sometimes this effort is physical - and it certainly involves more physical effort than philosophy - yet it also involves concentration, thought, deliberation and will power.[33]

The end product looks and feels effortless since it is efficient. But, as with most things in life, it can always be better. Asking more questions helps define where the process can be improved so that effort can be dedicated to making it better.

• • •

This entire book has been directed at hammer throwers and coaches. By now, I feel you must have a good understanding of the event. Therefore rather than leaving you with some parting words, I will instead direct them at your hammers. As astronaut John Glenn rocketed into space to become the first American ever to orbit Earth; his backup pilot Scott Carpenter passed along a few words of encouragement for him. The same can be said to your hammer: "Good luck, have a safe flight, and *Godspeed*."

REFERENCES AND CREDITS

Chapter 1
1. Raftery, Isolde. "Hammer Throw Becomes a Mystery." *New York Times*, 22 June 2010: B11.

Chapter 2
2. Jones, Max. "Revision of the Test Quadrathlon Tables." *Athletics Coach* 26.1 (1992): 27-29. The information can also be found online at <http://www.brianmac.co.uk/quad.htm>.
3. Bondarchuk, Anatoliy. *Transfer of Training in Sports Volume II*. Michigan: Ultimate Athlete Concepts, 2010. 141.
4. Bingisser, Martin. "Training Talk with Jüri Tamm (Part 2)." *HMMR Media*. 13 Dec. 2012. Web.

Chapter 3
This chapter was adapted from the article: Bingisser, Martin and Ryan Jensen. "Teaching the Hammer Throw: How to Get a Beginner to Throw in Just Days." *Track Coach* 194 (2011): 6191-6193.

5. For more information on the rules of hammer throwing, consult the IAAF Competition Rules published annually by the IAAF.

Chapter 5

6. Bartonietz, Klaus. "Hammer Throwing: Problems and Prospects." *Biomechanics in Sports*, Ed. Vladimir M. Zatsiorsky. London: Blackwell Science, 2000. 463.
7. Bartonietz (2000) 461.
8. Hunter, Iain (2005). "The Effect of Venue and Wind on the Distance of a Hammer Throw." *Research Quarterly for Exercise & Sport* 76.3 (2005): 347-351.
9. Mizera, Ferenc and Gabor Horvath. (2002). "Influence of Environmental Factors on Shot Put and Hammer Throw Range." *Journal of Biomechanics* 35.6 (2002): 785-796.
10. Isele, Regine, Luis Mendoza, and Eberhard Nixdorf. "Analyse Hammerwurf WM 2009 Berlin." *Olympiastützpunkt Hessen.* 2009. Web.

Chapter 6

11. Launder, Alan G., and John T. Gormley. *From Beginner to Bubka and Isinbayeva too!: An Australian Approach to Developing Pole Vaulters.* 2nd ed. Salem, Ore.: Your Town Press, 1997. 50.

Chapter 7

12. Bartonietz (2000): 466.
13. Bartonietz (2000): 462.

Chapter 8

14. Marra, Harry. "The Art of Coaching." United School of Sports, Zurich, Switzerland. 28 May 2013. Workshop.
15. Francis, Charlie. *Speed Trap: Inside the Biggest Scandal in Olympic History.* New York: St. Martin's Press, 1991. 31.
16. Gassner, Greg. "The Paradoxical Nature of the Hammer Throw." *Track Technique* 129 (1994): 4113-4114.

Chapter 9

This chapter was adapted from the article: Bingisser, Martin and Ryan Jen-

References & Credits

sen. "Teaching the Hammer Throw: Perfecting Technique." *Track Coach* 197 (2011): 6284-6286, 6292.

Chapter 10

17. Bartonietz 466.
18. Otto, Ralf. "NSA Photosequences 22-Hammer Throw Commentary." *New Studies in Athletics* 7.3 (1992): 51-65.
19. Dapena, Jesus. "Some biomechanical aspects of hammer throwing." *Athletics Coach* 23 (1989): 12-19.
20. Hildebrand, Falk and Klaus Bartonietz. "Eine Analyse der Technik des Hammerwerfens." Leipzig: Forschungsinstitut für Körperkultur und Sport (1995).
21. Bartonietz (2000): 470-471.
22. Bartonietz (2000): 472.
23. Sakr, Marwa. "Women's Hammer Throw: Measurement Information System and Kinetic Energy of Body Segments and Hammer Head." Diss. University of Konstanz. 2012.
24. Otto 63.
25. Murofushi, Koji, Shinji Sakurai, Junji Takamatsu and Koji Umegaki. "Hammer acceleration due to thrower and hammer movement patterns." *Sports Biomechanics* 6.3 (1997): 301-314.

Chapters 11-14

The following books provide a good overview of the theories of Dr. Anatoliy Bondarchuk:

- Bondarchuk, Anatoliy. *Transfer of Training in Sports*. Michigan: Ultimate Athlete Concepts, 2007.
- Bondarchuk, Anatoliy. *Transfer of Training in Sports Volume II*. Michigan: Ultimate Athlete Concepts, 2010.
- Bondarchuk, Anatoliy. *Long Term Training for Throwers*. Sydney: Australian Track and Field Coaches Association/Rothmans Foundation, 1994.
- Bondarchuk, Anatoliy. *Training Transfer in the Hammer Throw*. Kiev: Kamloops Track and Field Club, 2005.

Chapter 12

26. Bondarchuk (2010): 137-138.
27. Bondarchuk (2007): 111-112 and Bondarchuk (2005): 31.
28. Dapena (1989): 13.

Chapter 13

29. Bondarchuk (2007): 111-112 and Bondarchuk (2005) 31.
30. Bingisser, Martin. "On Short Hammers." *HMMR Media*. 28 Mar. 2013. Web.

Chapter 14

31. Balilionis, G, Nepocatych, S, Ellis, C. Richardson, M, Neggers, Y. and Bishop P. "Effects of different types of warm-up on swimming performance, reaction time, and dive distance." *Journal of Strength and Conditioning Research*. 26.12 (2012): 3297-3303.
32. Selye, Hans. *The Stress of Life*. Rev. Ed. New York: McGraw Hill, 1976.

Epilogue

33. Montero, Barbara Gail. "The Myth of 'Just Do It.'" *Opinionator*. New York Times. 9 June 2013.

ACKNOWLEDGEMENTS

Historian Henry Adams once said, "A teacher affects eternity; he can never tell where his influence stops." I am greatly indebted to the many people who have taught me about the hammer throw ,and this book is my attempt to help continue spreading that knowledge for eternity.

First and foremost, this book would not have been possible without the mentorship of Harold Connolly and Anatoliy Bondarchuk. In addition, coaches like Derek Evely, Glenn McAtee, Kevin McGill, Ryan Jensen, Zach Hazen, Vladimir Kevo, Sergey Litvinov, and dozens of others who have taken the time to explain to me what they do and why they do it. The list is too long to recite in full, but remembering all these people, I realize how fortunate I have been.

I am equally indebted to my family who have encouraged and supported my hammer throw addiction. My wife, parents, and siblings have all helped with this book both directly and indirectly through their work in editing and their support throughout my career.

ABOUT THE AUTHOR

G. Martin Bingisser is a Swiss-American hammer thrower and coach. He is currently the Swiss national champion, national hammer throw coach, as well as the hammer throwing coach for Leichtathletik-Club Zürich.

Born and raised in Seattle, Washington, Bingisser was first mentored in the hammer throw by former Olympic gold medalist Harold Connolly before attending the University of Washington. In 2005, he began training with former Soviet national coach Anatoliy Bondarchuk and quickly won two NCAA All-American honors and six Swiss national titles. Bingisser is also active in the education of coaches.

As founder of HMMR Media and the non-profit Evergreen Athletic Fund, he has worked on education and athlete support for more than a decade. In addition, he has been published in *New Studies in Athletics*, *Modern Athlete and Coach*, *Athletics Weekly*, *Leichtathletiktraining*, *Track Coach*, *American Track and Field*, as well as leading online publications such as *Juggernaut Training Systems* and *Elite FTS*.